Robert Hardy

THE WITCHES' PYRAMID

A Wiccan View of the Cabbala

BᵒA BIBLIOTHECA
ALEXANDRINA

First published as *The Witches' Pyramid* by Bibliotheca Alexandrina Ltd 2018
Copyright © Robert Hardy

Robert Hardy asserts the moral right to be identified as the author of this work.

ISBN 978-0-9933910-3-3
Cover and book design by Agnieszka Hulewicz

Contents

Excercises

Acknowledgements

Many thanks to Catherine Gregory for her early contributions in setting up this book. Thanks also to Dave Shirt for his time and work with the final edit. And thanks to my dear wife Jan for her love and patience.

Robert Hardy

Foreword

I was initiated into an Alexandrian coven in Bristol in 1971 and took to the Craft like a duck to water. After working hard for three years I hived off with my first wife Angela. Together we quickly formed a thriving group in Dursley. Sadly, as time went on, things did not work out between Angela and me, and the marriage broke up. I was left alone to run a coven with the help of its new initiates. In 1978 Jan arrived on the scene and quickly rose to the position of High Priestess. In 1984 Jan and I got married and together we ran the coven successfully. In 2017 Jan and I decided to retire from running a group and concentrate on running our local moot and supporting the local pagan community. All the experience and knowledge of a lifetime working with other like-minded people left me enriched, so through this book I hope to pass on some of my experiences with the ritual side of the Craft. There are many books published on Witchcraft and magic, explaining how to cast a circle, make a wand, call up the quarters etc. I hope this Witches' Pyramid will broaden the reader's horizons and take them deeper into the mysteries of the Western Tradition.

Witchcraft, the Tarot, and the Cabbala make strange bedfellows, but with a few subtle twists of the knobs, they can make very interesting ones. One of the things I find fascinating about the Tree of Life and its 22 connecting paths is the way you can place your own belief system and symbolism on them, thereby giving them a home. The beauty of doing this means that you can now cross reference your ideas with the Tree's existing symbolism, both religious and magical. Using the Tree as a pigeon-holing system will highlight the nuggets of gold in the debris of your own ego-driven fantasies. Out of the 22 paths on the Tree of Life I have concentrated on just six, those that make up the lower triangle, plus the lower Sephiroth. The pathworkings and experiences with the Sephiroth given you in this book are mainly of my own invention, built on my earlier explorations when working with inspirational teachers and friends.

To support the hermetic style of pathworkings (guided meditations), I have included exercises and magical practices to join the mental plane with that of the physical plane: "As Above, so Below".

I sincerely hope that you will find this book helpful when you construct your own pathworkings. Do not judge me too harshly; remember these pathworkings have evolved over the past 40 years or so, and have retained some of my earliest thoughts and dreams, as well as the later stuff. A mixture of old and new thinking: "Dust and Diamonds".

Robert Hardy

'Let me take you by the hand and show you a little truth, rather than a magnificent lie.' With these words I was led into the Temple of Malkuth:

The Temple of the Earth

The floor of the temple is constructed from smooth black and white tiles, much like a chessboard. Surrounding you stand ten black pillars, shot through with gold.

Beyond the circle of pillars is a thick morning mist, obscuring further vision.

In the centre of the temple stands a double cubic altar, upon which stands a single brass oil lamp, from which rises a bright white flame.

Looking up, you see that the tops of the pillars are enveloped in thick white mist which has a violet tinge to it. A small break appears in the mist, and for a second you glimpse a single star. Drawn back to the white flame on the altar, you are mesmerised by its simple beauty. As you stare deep into the heart of the flame, a shiver of excitement runs up your back as you realise that the flame is growing.

Larger and larger it grows, until it takes on a human shape. The air around you seems to vibrate as the form of the Archangel Sandalphon starts to materialise before your eyes.

Sandalphon is a female of ageless beauty. Her gown glows with the golden colours of autumn: citrine, olive, russet, and black. Her folded wings are as white as virgin snow. She smiles down on you and places her finger upon her lips in the sign of silence. You feel a compulsion to place the tip of your finger to your lips, and as you do so you lower your eyes from her gaze. Suddenly you fall, as if you have been dropped from a great height, and with a jolt you are back in your body, and the Temple of Malkuth has vanished.

Just thought you might like a lick of the spoon, before we start.

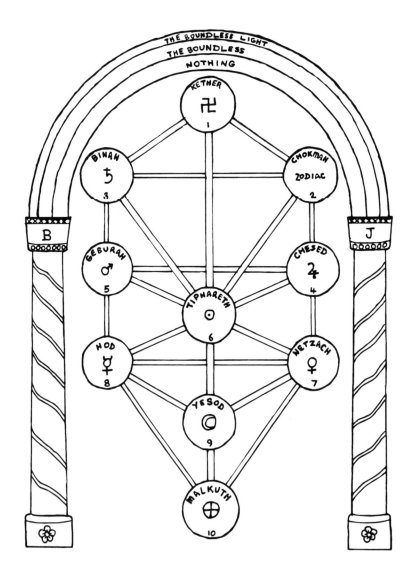

Figure 1. The Tree of Life.

Introduction

This book is a doorway into the fascinating world of the mystical Cabbala as seen from a Witch's point of view.

'The Witches' Pyramid' was a name adopted by West Country Witch covens in the early seventies; the name is still used to a lesser extent today. Detach the lower triangle from the rest of the Tree and visualise it in 3D. It forms a three-sided pyramid with Yesod at the top dominated by the Moon, hence the term 'the Witches' Pyramid'.

Note: the Witches' Pyramid also counts Malkuth as part of the lower triangle. This is a Wiccan adaptation; normally the Sephiroth Yesod, Hod and Netzach form the lower triangle and Malkuth (The Kingdom of Earth) stands alone, as if the element of Earth were in some way inferior to Fire, Water and Air. I believe that either the four elements stand together or not at all!

The Witches' Pyramid demonstrates and illuminates the lower triangle on the Tree of Life, containing all the fundamentals needed to give the initiate a firm grounding from which to work and, more importantly, understand their magic.

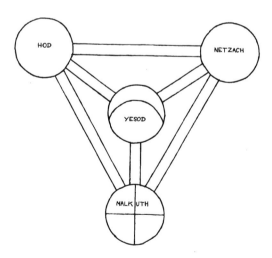

Figure 2. The Witches' Pyramid.

All Witches are Pagans.

But not all Pagans are Witches!

Now, in the second decade of the twenty-first century, many of the former practices of the modern Witch cult have been swamped by the ever-expanding phenomenon of western Paganism.

(I use the word 'Pagan' as a general blanket term. I am fully aware that many Pagans today identify themselves with other titles, such as Heathen, Norse tradition, Neo-Pantheist, etc.)

Paganism today is not dominated by Witchcraft, as it once was. Many Pagans prefer a more shamanic green path, being at one with nature, and have little or no interest in witchcraft, ritual magic, or the Cabbala.

Unfortunately this also seems to be the case with a number of new wave Wiccan groups, who it seems have turned their back on ceremonial magic altogether, opting instead for a more worship-based ideology, with a bit of healing on the side, and with little or no serious magical work employed.

What used to set witches apart from Pagans in general was their use and understanding of magic.

So, with this in mind, I hope this book will rekindle your interest and bewitch you into dusting off your old magical Grimoires.

1. Introduction

These books and magics and metaphysics
are heavenly!

Ten things to consider about the Western Cabbalistic Tradition:

1. The Cabbalistic Tree of Life should be as important to the modern enlightened Witch as the four quarters and the circle are.
2. Do not underestimate the power of the Tree of Life as a learning tool; to do so will diminish your ability to fully embrace your magical work.
3. Fear not! Studying the Cabbala will not steal you away from your chosen Wiccan path like a thief in the night. Quite the opposite: it will illuminate and reinforce your belief structure.
4. Truth! Many of the ritual gestures, signs and sigils used in Witchcraft today can be traced back to the Cabbala-based practices of magical lodges, such as the Golden Dawn and similar magical schools of the nineteenth and early twentieth century.
5. In the world of ritual magic, the westernised form of the Cabbala is one of the few complete magical systems in existence today. Most other systems are incomplete and potentially dangerous to beginners and experts alike.
6. The Cabbalistic Tree of Life is ancient. Many believe that it and the Tree that grew in the Garden of Eden, with its tempting serpent and forbidden fruit, are one and the same.
7. Alice's looking glass; the enchanted wardrobe leading to Narnia; Frodo's precious ring. All these are portals to mysterious worlds full of enchantment and magic. The Cabbala offers you a chance to enter a world no less captivating.

8. The twenty two Major Arcana (greater mysteries) of Tarot are called keys. With such keys you can open, one by one, each of the twenty two paths on the Cabbalistic Tree of Life, which will enrich your magical practice in many unexpected ways.

9. The Cabbalist embraces the idea of the Great Work, which means, in a nut-shell: if you strive towards the light, you will help elevate the group soul of humankind up to a higher plane of existence; the very act of your magical work causes spiritual evolution. On the other hand, if everyone looks only to the material gutter, humankind is doomed.

10.   Magical development is ten percent devotion and ninety percent bloody hard work.

Initiation and the Tree of Life

Behind the secretive doors of the great magical lodges, Magicians employed a ten degree initiatory system based on the ten Sephiroth.

Starting at the bottom of the Tree with Malkuth, they would first be initiated to the grade of Earth. With subsequent initiations they would work their way up the Tree to the grand title of Ipsissimus, based on the mysterious Sephiroth Kether.

Wicca has only three degrees, but, as is the case with their magical cousins in the temple lodges, the Witches' degree system is based on the Tree of Life.

I have set out below the three degrees of the Wiccan system and their association with the respective Sephiroth. I feel it is important to point out this underlying connection between Witchcraft and the Cabbala, to reinforce its continued use in the Craft.

The First Degree

The triangle is used to symbolise the grade of First Degree. It is called the grade of the inverted triangle, which covers the spheres of Netzach, Hod and Malkuth with Yesod in the centre: the Witches' Pyramid.

The Second Degree

This uses the symbol of the pentagram. It is called the grade of the inverted pentagram, which covers the spheres of Malkuth, Hod, Netzach, Tiphareth, Geburah and Gedulah.

The Third Degree

This uses the symbols of both the pentagram and the triangle. It is called the grade of the pentagram and triangle, which cover the spheres of Malkuth, Yesod, Hod, Netzach, Tiphareth, Geburah, Gedulah, Binah, Chokmah and Kether.

Once the initiate has reached Third Degree, they would be expected to have a reasonable knowledge of all ten Sephiroth and their 22 connecting paths.

Again, the reason I have explained this idea in detail is to illustrate that, like it or not, the Cabbala is an integral part of the fabric of modern Witchcraft. And, if you're not being taught the fundamentals of Cabbalistic magic and the Tree of Life, reading this book will make you the first working Cabbalist of your group.

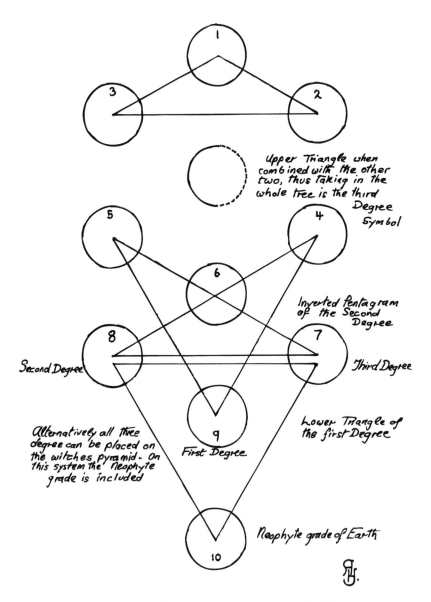

Upper Triangle when combined with the other two, thus taking in the whole Tree is the third Degree Symbol

Inverted Pentagram of the Second Degree

Second Degree

Third Degree

Lower Triangle of the first Degree

First Degree

Alternatively all three degree can be placed on the witches pyramid. On this system the Neophyte grade is included

Neophyte grade of Earth

Figure 3. The Wiccan degree system on the Tree.

2. As Above, So Below

One significant principle in magical arts is the celebrated Hermetic maxim: 'As Above, So Below', which is a shortened, modern version of 'That which is below corresponds to that which is above, and that which is above corresponds to that which is below, to accomplish the miracle of the One Thing'.

According to magical legend, those words were engraved on a large emerald tablet that fell to earth from the crown of Lucifer – which is now housed in the Temple of Venus, and which you will find in the Sephirah Netzach.

Another widely held belief is that the emerald tablet (also called Tabula Smaragdina) was found in a stone tomb along with the corpse of Hermes Trismegistus. It was said to be inscribed in Phoenician, with all the magical secrets of the universe. It was translated into Latin in the thirteenth century from some earlier Arabic versions. It's interesting that Trismegistus means Thrice Great; perhaps it refers to 'three times initiated'!

'As Above, So Below' is a message quite simple, but incredibly profound. In its purest form, its meaning is clear to all who practice Astrology. "Above" is the starry vault of heaven. "Below" lies the Earth we live on.

One of the earliest-held beliefs of humankind is that the stars hold the key to our personal destiny. Was not Stonehenge erected to monitor the movements of the planets and stars, and to map out the year into divisions for husbandry and religious festival?

If Venus enters your sign in the heavens, and the time is right, romantic involvements will ensue. As above, so below.

This is why magicians invoke and work with the planets and constellations: in the hope they can dampen down their worst effects, and encourage their beneficial natures. (Remember that anyone who works

15

magic is by definition a magician, and that includes witches.)

However, Cabbalisticly speaking, the maxim 'As Above, So Below' refers to the idea that 'As above' is the Macrocosm: the vast "out there" that embraces infinity, and which many choose to call God. And then there's the microcosm: 'So below', which is the macrocosm, mirrored in your own small physical self. Therefore, every human being is a mini representation of the universe and everything in it, which in the world of the Cabbala is represented by the microcosmic concept of Adam/ Eve Kadmon translated as Heavenly Man and Heavenly Woman.

God made man in his own image?

Figure 4. Yod he vau he as the image of Man.

This principle is fully explored by superimposing the image of the Tree of Life directly over the human body. Once there, it is called 'Adam Kadmon' (Heavenly Man) or 'Eve Kadmon' (Heavenly Woman). This

16

concept is important because as you explore the various paths and Sephiroth on the Tree of Life, microcosmically speaking you are also exploring your own inner paths.

It's on this inner level that all the subtle changes take place. These changes go on to manifest themselves in your everyday life, making you a stronger and better person.

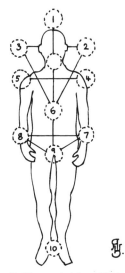

Figure 5. Eve and Adam Kadmon.

The Sephiroth

Before you can move on to the pathworkings, you should first familiarise yourself with the ten Sephiroth. As you read through the text, just let the words wash over you. They will imprint themselves in your mind with little exertion on your part, for they are already within you!

Real power is invisible.

That's what makes it invincible.

KETHER

- The first Sephirah on the Tree of Life.
- Translation: 'the Crown'.
- Colour: white light.
- Astrological: the source of energy from the infinite Un-manifest.
- Kether sits on the top of the Pillar of the Mildness.

Look up into the night sky on a clear night; look up past the roofs of the houses, up past the top branches of the trees. Let yourself be one with the stars. Now concentrate on the velvet blackness between them. The ancients believed that behind that veil of darkness, hidden from mortal eyes, was the mystery of God. This is what Kether represents: the inexplicable one eternal force behind the force.

All that has happened and all that will happen resides there, beyond the concept of time and space. Imagine a full orchestra assembled in a concert hall, about to play a well-known piece of classical music. The conductor taps gently on the lectern and lifts the baton, and the hall falls silent as if under a spell. In those few moments of silence before the baton falls and the music starts, the whole essence of the musical composition is focused. Nothing has happened, and yet everything has happened. That moment is the enigma which is Kether.

CHOKMAH

- The second Sephirah on the Tree of Life.
- Translation: 'Wisdom'.
- Colour: milky grey.
- Astrological symbol: the Zodiac.
- Chokmah sits at the top right hand pillar, the Pillar of Mercy.

Here is the first movement, and with movement comes energy. This energy is the first positive. One of the symbols of Chokmah is the erect phallus, because on an abstract level Chokmah is the Supernal Father. His phallus ejaculates star dust like sperm into the womb of Binah, the Supernal Mother, and through restriction she moulds the dust into stars.

BINAH
- The third Sephirah on the Tree of Life.
- Translation: 'Understanding'.
- Colour: black.
- Planet: Saturn.
- Binah sits on top of the left hand pillar, the Pillar of Severity.

As the phallus is symbolic of Chokmah, it is logical that the Yoni is symbolic of Binah, and this is indeed the case. Binah is the third Sephirah, and the number three can form a simple triangle, which confines the space inside it. As more of the nebulous stellar dust is drawn into Binah's great womb of space, it is consolidated into universal energy. It is Binah the Great Mother who gives birth to the universe.

It is little wonder then that the 14th path that connects Chokmah and Binah together is represented by the tarot card The Empress, and pictured on that card is an enthroned pregnant queen or Goddess.

These first three Sephiroth, Kether, Chokmah, and Binah, make up the Supernal Triangle at the top of the Tree of Life.

CHESED
Leaving the Supernal Triangle we move down the Tree to the fourth Sephirah, Chesed.
- Translation: 'Mercy'.
- Colour: blue.
- Planet: Jupiter.
- Chesed is located on the left hand Pillar of Mercy.

We have now entered the Ethical Triangle. Chesed is the great designer: taking the energy from Binah he will create the model for citadels, towns, temples, cities, and all the trappings of civilisation. At this point they are just concepts. They will not become dependable and solid until they have been built in the world of Malkuth, the kingdom of the material. Yet if their blueprint had not been set out in Chesed in the first place, they could never have been built in Malkuth.

GEBURAH

- Geburah is the fifth Sephirah.
- Translation: 'Strength'.
- Colour: red.
- Planet: Mars.
- Geburah is located on the right hand Pillar of Severity.

If Chesed is the Lord of Creation, then Geburah is the Lord of Destruction. Geburah's job is to break down outdated modes, to make way for new ideas and concepts. For a great city to grow to its full potential, it will have to stand on the remnants of the past. You need to clear the way for the new; if you don't, you run the risk of stagnation and decay. So, to put it simply, if Chesed builds up, Geburah seeks to tear down. I must stress that Geburah is not an evil force: Geburah destroys unbalanced energy that is considered to be corrupt, undesirable or outdated. The danger here is that if we are afraid to change and realize our full potential, we could fall into this latter category and become prey to the sword of Mars!

TIPHARETH

- Tiphareth is the sixth Sephirah.
- Translation: 'Beauty'.
- Colour: Golden Yellow.
- Planet: The Sun.
- Tiphareth is located on the middle Pillar of Mildness.

The two Sephiroth Chesed and Geburah, with their runaway nature, need to be kept in check. This is achieved by the sixth Sephirah

Tiphareth through the power of love and compassion. Tiphareth sits in the centre of the Tree of Life, on the middle pillar. It brings harmony and balance to the individual Sephiroth that stand about it, much like our own Sun sits at the centre of our solar system creating harmony. Tiphareth is the approachable face of Kether, revealed on a lower plane in the guise of the Son of God. You could argue that his mother is the Supernal Binah, which would mean that Tiphareth is the son of the Goddess.

Tiphareth is also associated with sacrificed Gods, who represent the personal sacrifice we must make if we wish to embrace Tiphareth fully. By sacrificing our personality (ego), which we believe to be our real selves, we rediscover our inner Sun child.

To recap, Tiphareth is symbolic of our higher self, but a higher self that we can commune with, full of love and divine grace. Tiphareth also has the ability to harnesses the power of Geburah and Chesed for the benefit of universal balance.

NETZACH

We now leave the Ethical Triangle and move down the Tree to encounter the third and last triangle, the Astral Triangle.

- The first Sephirah on the Astral Triangle is Netzach, the seventh Sephirah.
- Translation: 'Victory'.
- Colour: green.
- Planet: Venus.
- Netzach is located at the bottom of the Pillar of Mercy.

As the energy of Kether moves down the Tree from Sephirah to Sephirah, the individual power of each Sephirah flows into the one below like a champagne fountain. Now we have reached Netzach, the seventh Sephirah, the combined energies from all the above Sephiroth make Netzach a rich soup. And rich indeed are the powers of Netzach, with Venus as its mundane planet. Netzach is associated with the group souls of all the creatures of the earth, along with the much older soul of the plant kingdom – not yet manifest on the physical plane of blood and muscle, bough and leaf (which is only possible in Malkuth), but on an emotional level of instinct and gut feeling, plus raw passion.

HOD

- Hod is the eighth Sephirah.
- Translation: 'Splendour'.
- Colour: orange.
- Planet: Mercury.
- Hod is located at the bottom of the Pillar of Severity.

In many ways, Hod is opposite to Netzach: where Netzach is fiery and emotional, Hod is cold and intellectual. Hod is the Sephirah of science and language. The planet associated with Hod is Mercury, the Messenger of the Gods. The power of speech resides in Hod. That power of communication that we take so often for granted is one of the things responsible for elevating the human kind to such highs. However, for all the intellectual might of Hod, the pull of wild nature and the pipes of Pan are never far away.

YESOD

- Yesod is the ninth Sephirah.
- Translation: 'Foundation'.
- Colour: violet.
- Planet: The Moon.
- Yesod is located on the middle Pillar of Mildness, so, as you would expect, Yesod helps balance the two Sephiroth above (Netzach and Hod).

Yesod completes the last triangle; Yesod's sphere of operation is in the Astral light which underlies all cyclic forces of matter. Yesod is placed on the middle pillar of the Tree between Tiphareth and Malkuth like a double facing mirror. Yesod shines with the reflected light of Tiphareth above, yet absorbs the hope, fears and dreams of humankind who reside below in Malkuth.

It is in Yesod that the Astral Sea can be found, where dwells all – fantastic images one can dream of. The beautiful and the grotesque reside there. The Astral light is also known as The Akashic Fluid, the fifth element. We are all familiar with the four elements of Fire, Water, Air and Earth which operate in Malkuth; through interaction with Yesod you will become familiar with this fifth element, the Astral light. The Astral light is neither physical nor spiritual; it is somewhere between the two. It is pliable in its nature; if you or any other creature of intelligent will thinks of an image, the Astral light will be only too happy to model it for you. Some say you can actually see the Astral light in the dark, made up of millions of points of light, often dismissed by the scientists with a vague reference to neurological sensation.

When those points of light are gathered and shaped together in a human form by a temporal memory, locked perhaps into the fabric of a building, someone gets a fright, whilst the local newspaper reports lurid tales of haunting. The scientists scream that there no such things as ghosts: 'when you're dealing with Yesod, all things are possible'.

The Moon is the mundane planet of Yesod, and is the perfect example of how Yesod functions. The Moon appears to wax and wane from New to Full and back again. The light from the Moon does indeed wax and wane, but the Moon's mass is constant, so the effect is illusory. Many things about Yesod are also illusory: it not called 'the treasure house of images' for nothing. The Moon is responsible for the ebbing and flowing of the oceans, and without this constant ebbing and flowing, life as we know it would not have evolved on Earth at all. The Moon is the great spoon that stirs the cauldron, and the Sun holds the handle.

MALKUTH
- Malkuth is the tenth Sephirah on the Tree of Life.
- Translation: 'the Kingdom'.

- Colours: citrine, olive, russet, and black.
- Planet: The Earth on which we walk.
- Malkuth sits at the bottom of the Pillar of Mildness.

We have reached the last of the Sephirah on the Tree of Life, or the first one, depending on which way you are travelling. If you start at the Temple of Malkuth and travel up the Tree of Life, you are following the Path of the Serpent; the path of the initiate. However, if you start at Kether and travel down the Tree of Life, as we have just done, you will be following the path of the lightning bolt, sometimes called the path of the shining sword; the path of devotion.

Malkuth is the world we are born into, the world of the four elements, and is set apart from the other nine Sephiroth. Malkuth is the crowning glory of the Tree of Life. It is the final conclusion: 'the physical universe, everything from nothing!'

Matter is the spiritual orgasm of the Godhead, flowing out endlessly in an ecstasy of creation, like fruit from the Amalthean Horn (Horn of Plenty). This is made possible because Kether feeds Malkuth, and likewise Malkuth feeds Kether. To quote the hermetic axiom again, 'as above, so below'. This is a little like the Ouroborus, the snake that devours itself, and sustains itself thereby.

The divine nature of Kether can be seen in every flower, every grain of sand, in all things. As a result, this power must also reside in me and you. Man is God and God is Man, or Woman is the Goddess and the Goddess is Woman. This is one of the great mysteries of Malkuth.

To conclude this section on the Ten Sephiroth, I would like to leave you with an old Tantric quote to meditate on: 'God is Sex'.

3. The Path of the Serpent

Adam/Eve Kadmon

Let's look at how the ten Sephiroth bed in to your microcosmic Body of Light, which we will now refer to as Adam or Eve Kadmon, depending on your gender.

The elongated form of the Tree of Life fits well over the human body; perhaps this is why it is said that God made Man in His own image. Men and women are mirrors of the macrocosm, the great whole, the universe.

All the powers of the universe, both hidden and exposed, are reflected on to the convex face of your Akashic egg (a Hindu term for the all-pervading field of ether, in which a record of past events is imprinted). The sum total of this information is enormous, and our ability to embrace this knowledge is limited to our own inner development, which is effected by our Karma. In the teachings of the Cabbala, it is taught that Man and Woman are the Tree of Life, being a microcosmic facsimile of the principles found on the macrocosmic Tree.

The Adam and Eve Kadmon exercise I have given at the end of the chapter will help you explore your own bodily Tree of Life. Search and examine it with care, with a view to discovering the true potential of this new-found knowledge.

Here is a brief description of the Sephiroth and their positions on your body. I have decided to start at your feet, Malkuth, and work back up the body to the top of your head, Kether. This is called The Path of the Serpent.

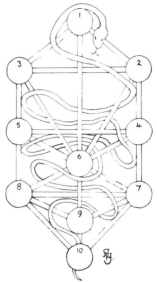

Figure 6. The Path of the Serpent.

Malkuth

Malkuth is under the soles of your feet; you are standing on it. It is seen as a quartered circle made up of the four autumn colours: citrine, olive, russet, and black. Malkuth affects the feet and ankles and has some influence over your legs. Malkuth's authority decreases quickly as you move up your legs towards your lower torso and genital zone.

Yesod

Your Yesod zone is situated in and around your genital and anus area, and is seen as a violet spinning disc. It is active mainly between the thighs and just above the pubic line, and its influence does not extend to the outer hips. If however you are in a state of sexual arousal its power will extend upwards along the spinal column and outwards to Hod and Netzach, thus extending its range. In this form the energy is called the Kundalini; like anything to do with sex it is very addictive. You have been warned! (Kundalini is latent sexual energy believed to lay

26

coiled around the base of the spine. It is Sanskrit for 'snake'.)

The middle pillar on the Tree of Life passes through Yesod and Tiphareth and extends to the top of your head, Kether. This midway line is also called the Pillar of Mildness.

Hod

The Hod zone sits on the right-hand side of the pelvis (right hip) and is seen as an orange spinning disc. Hod also has some influence over your right leg, because in some rituals it is symbolic of the right-hand pillar of the Tree of Life (the Pillar of Severity). Again, the influence decreases quickly as you move down the leg to Malkuth.

Netzach

The Netzach zone is on the opposite side of your body and sits on the left-hand side of the pelvis (left hip), and is seen as a green spinning disc. Netzach also has some influence over your left leg, because in some rituals involving the use of the microcosmic tree it is symbolic of the left-hand pillar of the Tree of Life (the Pillar of Mercy). Again, the influence decreases quickly as you move down the leg.

Once Yesod, Hod and Netzach have been activated you will have formed your first triangle of manifestation.

Tiphareth

The Tiphareth zone is located on the middle pillar just under the ribcage. This spot is called the solar plexus. It is seen as a golden spinning disc. Its influence also extends to the general heart region, lungs, and upper middle torso.

Geburah

The Geburah zone is located on your right shoulder, and is seen as a red spinning disc. Its power extends down the right arm. If you imagine yourself as an angel your right arm would become your right wing (the Red Wing of Geburic power).

Chesed

Chesed is located on the opposite left shoulder and is seen as a blue spinning disc. It also extends down the left arm. Similarly, if you imagine yourself as an angel, your left arm would become your left wing (the Blue Wing of Chesedic compassion).

Once Tiphareth, Geburah and Chesed have been activated you have your second triangle of manifestation.

Binah

Next is Binah, the Great Mother. The Binah centre is located on the right side of the head at the temple, and is seen as a spinning disc of jet black. Its energy extends into the right-hand side of your aura.

Chokmah

Next is Chokmah, the Great Father. The Chokmah centre is located on the left side of the head at your temple, and is seen as a shining disc of grey light. Its energy extends into the left-hand side of your aura. When Binah and Chokmah unite they are similar to the Yin and Yang symbol: each has the seed of the other at its heart.

Kether

Kether sits above the top of your head like a crown of white candle flames in the shape of Yods.

Well, there you have it: your microcosmic body represented as The Tree of Life. To help you better understand its subtle power, now try the Adam/Eve Kadmon exercise set out below.

Before we try the Adam and Eve Kadmon exercise, study figure 1 and 2, paying particular attention to the different colours. You will need to visualise them in the coming exercise. Find a quiet place to perform the Adam/Eve Kadmon exercise. It should be clean and cleansed; joss sticks are fine, salt water should be sprinkled, and flowers are always a nice touch.

The Adam and Eve Kadmon Exercise

Imagine that you are standing on a large disc divided into four quarters, upon which lie autumn leaves. This will act as your sphere of Malkuth. Black, olive, russet, and citrine are the four colours traditionally associated with the tenth Sephirah Malkuth, on the Queen scale.

(There are four different colour scales associated with the Tree of Life: the King scale, the Queen scale, the Knight scale, and the Princess scale. With this type of magical working we always use the Queen colour scale.)

These four colours are reflected in the autumn leaves. The four winds that represent the four quarters of the Earth spin around the disc of Earth, lifting the leaves and spinning them up into the air, and coiling around your legs like a whirlwind. The spinning power of Malkuth spirals up your legs until it touches your Yesodic point, your genitalia.

Visualise a flare of violet light expanding into a spinning disc. Touch this spot on your body with your mind, and be conscious of your own sexuality.

Now activate your Hod and Netzach centres, imagining Hod on your right hip as a spinning disc of orange light.

Now activate Netzach on your left hip, an emerald green spinning disc of light.

Yesod, Hod and Netzach are now invoked, forming your first triangle of power - or the first cup of the crucible - that you will now fill with Odic energy.

Concentrate on your genital centre, wherein sleeps the serpent of the Kundalini. Now, awaken this sleeping power and fill this divine triangle with Odic force. Let your inner serpent that lies dormant at the bottom of your spine open its eyes and uncoil to fill this triangle with its energy, which will begin to vibrate with power. When you feel suitably aroused sexually, you can go on to the next stage. You can no longer contain all this force: it is pushing to move up, so let it do so. Slowly the force rises up past the pelvic zone, forming into the head of a snake. Reaching up, it touches your Tiphareth centre at your solar plexus, striking at its heart like a viper.

The golden light of Tiphareth flares out, embracing and absorbing this current of energy and growing in size like the rising Sun. Now visualise the spheres of Geburah and Chesed shining bright red on the right shoulder and bright blue on the left shoulder. This forms your second triangle, which you slowly fill with the golden yellow light of Tiphareth. Feed it all the time from below. When your second triangle is full of golden spiritual love, let the power rise up naturally through the neck and through the back of the head, to reach the centre of the forehead. Visualise Binah and Chokmah positioned each side of your head at the temples. Taking power from below, they will grow and revolve. Binah will appear as a disc of shining black light, Chokmah a shining disc of grey light. Binah and Chokmah seem to call to one another forming a link resembling a cosmic ribbon, formed like a figure-of-eight set horizontally, this ancient infinity symbol vibrating and crossing the third eye.

Then see a spinning crown of brilliant white Hebrew Yods descend from above to alight on your brow. You are now at one with the cosmos: a huge towering figure, with your feet on the earth and your head in the stars.

I hope you enjoyed the Adam/Eve Kadmon experience. You do not need to close the Sephiroth, which you would do when working with your Chakras. However, it is wise to ground yourself on leaving your sacred space. There are many ways to accomplish this, and I will give you three. Carry out all three one after the other and you will be fine:

Imagine your crown of Yods ascending from your brow into the heavens. Then absorb the rest of the Sephiroth deep into your body.

Concentrating on your Malkuth zone, feel the four-quartered disc of the Earth under the soles of your feet. Then vibrate the word of power attributed to Malkuth which is Adonai ha-Aretz (Lord of the Earth).

Number three is the simplest of the lot: have something to eat and drink that will ground you nicely.

4. Tarot Cards, Hebrew Letters,

and the Cabbalistic Cross

There is no religion higher than Truth.

Of Tarot Cards and Letters

A pack of tarot cards is an essential collaborator in the Cabbalist's arsenal. Each of the twenty-two paths on the Tree of Life have a trump card (Major Arcanum) assigned to it; these are the path's keys. Each of the ten Sephiroth have four suit cards (Minor Arcana) assigned to them. For example Malkuth is the tenth Sephiroth so has the four tens assigned to it; the ten of Wands, the ten of Cups, the ten of Swords, and the ten of Pentacles. Yesod would have the four nines, and so on up the Tree.

In each set, the cards represent the four elements, which in turn reflect the four-fold nature of their particular Sephirah. Fire is Wands, Water is Cups, Air is Swords, and Earth is Pentacles.

The appropriate card allocated to any path gives an insight into the nature of that path. For example the 25th path from Yesod to Tiphareth has Temperance assigned to it. Temperance is one of the trumps (Major Arcana). Pictured on the card is an angel pouring liquid from one chalice into another. One chalice is made of silver and the other gold. Yesod is associated with the Moon (silver), and Tiphareth is associated with the Sun (gold). So you could say that the lesson of the path is to blend the Solar and Lunar energy in yourself, thus allowing you to raise up through the veil to the next level.

Figure 7. The tarot card 'Temperance'.

Temperance is also a card of patience, and you will need to be patient before you can move out of the Witches' Pyramid, because first you must learn all its lessons.

Let's look at the major tarot cards and their locations on the 22 paths.

Tarot Cards on the Connecting Paths

- 11th path: The Fool
- 13th path: The High Priestess
- 15th path: The Emperor
- 17th path: The Lovers
- 19th path: Strength
- 21st path: The Wheel of Fortune
- 23rd path: The Hanged Man
- 25th path: Temperance

- 12th path: The Magician
- 14th path: The Empress
- 16th path: The Hierophant
- 18th path: The Chariot
- 20th path: The Hermit
- 22nd path: Justice
- 24th path: Death
- 26th path: The Devil

Witches' Pyramid

- 27th path: The Tower
- 29th path: The Moon
- 31st path: Judgment
- 28th path: The Star
- 30th path: The Sun
- 32th path: The Universe

As well as the tarot cards, each of the twenty-two paths also has a Hebrew letter assigned to it. To travel your chosen path you will need to be able to visualise its Hebrew letter, so practice of drawing the letters is never a waste of time.

The Hebrew alphabet is a sacred alphabet because the ancient priests believed that each letter expresses a small insight into the nature of their God. As in the Roman alphabet, each Hebrew letter also represents a number, so given sets of numbers spell out divine or demonic names. This practice led to many coded talismans and hidden magical formulae, which gave rise to the legend of the occult (secret) nature of early magicians.

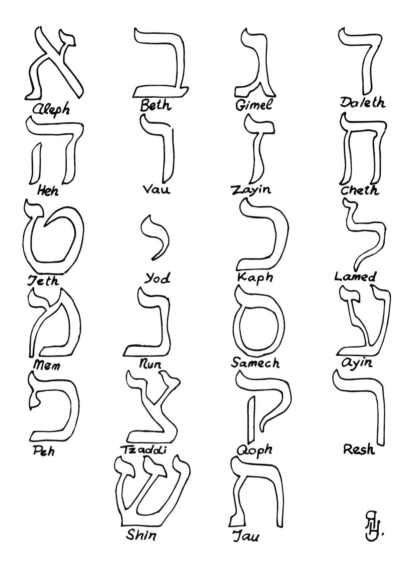

Figure 8. The 22 letters of the Hebrew alphabet.

34

The Hebrew letter assigned to any given path acts to energize that path. The letters are located at the path's halfway point, which metaphorically separates the path into two. As a result, the letter is positioned where the powers of the opposing Sephiroth should be in balance.

For the purpose of this book you will only need to scrutinize the letters and cards found on the lower triangle, the Witches' Pyramid. Obviously it would be unwise not to be familiar with the remaining letters and tarot cards, but it's the six paths which make up the lower triangle that we will be working with.

In the pursuit of magical excellence we talk a lot about balance, balancing things up, being in balance, the principle of Yin and Yang.

In the world of engineering, if a part of a machine is out of balance, it will eventually tear itself to bits. When you took your first tottering steps you fell over again and again until you mastered your sense of balance; luckily you were nearer the ground back then. So clearly you would be unwise to venture into the unknown without first being in balance. One excellent way of balancing both your mental and spiritual energies is an exercise called 'The Cabbalistic Cross'.

The Cabbalistic Cross is similar to the Adam and Eve Kadmon exercise, but does not employ all ten Sephiroth. Despite this it is a well-known balancing ritual. Numerous magicians and witches perform it in the eastern quarter as part of their opening rubrics.

The Cabbalistic Cross

Properly prepare your space and stand facing east, feet together, arms folded over your chest forming an X.

Unfold your arms and raise your hands over your head. Let the fingers and thumbs of both hands form a triangle, fingers pointing up as in the triangle. Imagine the white fire from the universe materializing in this triangle.

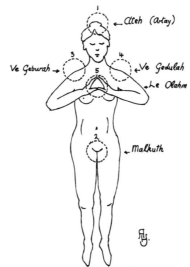

Figure 9. The Cabbalistic Cross on the body.

Next bring your hands down over your forehead with the tips of your fingers still pointing up, to form the triangle of Fire, and vibrate the word "Ateh".

Visualise a spinning disc of white light on your forehead.

Next bring your hands down and place them over your genital area, this time with the tips of your fingers pointing down to form the triangle of Earth, and vibrate the word "Malkuth".

Then visualise the power of Malkuth rushing up from the floor to sit in your hands in the form of a radiant spinning disc of autumn colours.

Next bring your hands up and across to your right shoulder, fingers pointing up to form the triangle of Air. Vibrate the words "Ve-Geburah", and visualise a spinning disc of red light.

Next move your hands across to your left shoulder, fingers pointing up to form the triangle of Water. Vibrate the words "Ve-Gedulah", and visualise a spinning disc of blue light.

Then finally clasp your hands over your heart and vibrate the words "le-olam", and visualise a golden light streaming through your fingers from your heart centre. This brings the exercise to a finish.

Let's go through what we have done in detail. Clearly the finished result of this exercise is to mark out on your body the sign of the Calvary cross. This was one of the reasons why the Cabbalistic Cross was so popular with magicians early in the twentieth century, because most of them were heavily influenced by Christianity. Furthermore they believed that the sign of the Calvary cross protected them from evil influences. However, whether or not you agree with this doctrine is a matter of personal belief. Crosses in all their many forms, including the Calvary cross, were used as religious and magical symbols long before Christianity had made its debut on the religious stage.

Jesus Christ was crucified on a wooden cross for claiming that man was part divine: "I am the Son of God". This ties in well with the Cabbalistic view that man is made in God's image. The words spoken in the Cabbalistic Cross reinforce your individual divinity, and the concept that you are a god or goddess in the making.

'Ateh' is the first word you utter after bringing the power down upon your forehead. It's this word that puts a whole new slant on what the ritual is really about. At first you could be forgiven in thinking that the Cabbalistic Cross is a prayer to the one God. In fact I believe that it's a prayer to yourself: your own individual godhood!

If we translate the words of the Cabbalistic Cross into English, the point I am trying to make will become clear:
'Ateh' (touching forehead) English translation 'I Am'. (That's you!)
'Malkuth' (touching genitals) English translation 'The Kingdom'.
'Ve-Geburah' (touching right shoulder) English translation 'The Power'.
'Ve-Gedulah' (touching left shoulder) English translation 'The Glory'.
'Le-olam' (clasping hands at breast level) English translation 'For Ever'.

The first words the magician utters are 'I AM', so what the magician or witch is doing is reinforcing the belief that man or woman has the potential to aspire to divinity.

The connection between the Cabbalistic Cross and the Calvary cross is plain to see. Let's move away from Christian ideology to a more classical Pagan theme. I would like you to consider the similarity between the Caduceus and the Cabbalistic Cross. (The Caduceus is the herald's staff carried by the Greek messenger-god Hermes, equivalent to the Roman Mercury). Aleister Crowley makes the assumption that the Caduceus and the magician are one and the same. (See the tarot card 'The Magus' in Aleister Crowley's celebrated Thoth pack for more insight.)

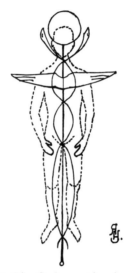

Figure 9. The Caduceus placed on the body.

Before I close this section on the Cabbalistic Cross I have included the full ritual of the Cabbalistic Cross.

Full Ritual of the Cabbalistic Cross

Start as usual in the eastern quarter and perform the Cabbalistic Cross. When you have finished, remain were you are, stand with your feet together and hands clasped over your breast, and say:
"BEFORE ME RAPHAEL"

Then say:
"BEHIND ME GABRIEL"
Stretch out your right arm to the south and say:
"ON MY RIGHT HAND MICHAEL"
*Leave your right hand were it is. Next stretch out your left hand to
the north and say:*
"ON MY LEFT HAND AURIEL"
*You will now be standing with both arms outstretched. Next point
your fingers up with your palms facing north and south and say:*
"AROUND ME FLAME THE PENTAGRAMS"
Now stretch your arms up above your head and say:
"IN THE COLUMN STANDS THE SIX-RAYED STAR"
*Next let your fingers and thumbs form a triangle, fingers pointing up
as in the triangle. Now perform the Cabbalistic Cross again:*
'Ateh' (touching forehead).
'Malkuth' (touching genitals).
'Ve-Geburah' (touching right shoulder).
'Ve-Gedulah' (touching left shoulder).
'Le-olam' (clasping hands at breast level).
Finishing with the words:
'Forever and ever amen'.

This concludes Chapter 4. You will need to learn the Cabbalistic Cross
off by heart, as you will execute it before each pathworking session. If
you're not happy about using the word 'amen' because of its Christian
associations, remember that some scholars think that the word origi-
nated from the name of the Egyptian God Amon, king of all Gods, later
united with the Sun God Ra to become Amon-Ra. When the Israelites
left Egypt they must have taken with them a large slice of Egyptian religious and magical modi operandi, which we may allow ourselves to believe is hidden deep in the Cabbala, along with other ancient mysteries.

5. Angels and Temples

I can call upon the spirits from the vasty

deep! Yes, and so can any man, but will

they come when you call them?

Angels

Meeting and working with angelic beings on the Tree of Life is paramount to your pathworking experiences, because the first being you will encounter when you step into the Temple of Malkuth will be the archangel Sandalphon.

What exactly is an angel?

'Angel' is from the Greek *angelos*, 'messenger'. According to the *Concise Oxford English Dictionary*, it is 'a spiritual being believed to act as an attendant or messenger of God, conventionally represented a being of human form with wings; a person of great beauty, kindness, or virtue.' And who am I to disagree with the *Oxford Dictionary*?

Figure 10. The Angel Sandalphon. [Combined with fig. 11, p. 43]

5. Angels and Temples

When working on the Tree of Life you will encounter many angelic orders, in fact angels inhabit every nook and cranny of the Tree.

There are ten spheres on the Tree of Life, and each Sephirah is assigned an order of angels, plus an archangel to lead them. I have listed them below: read through them a few times to familiarise yourself with their names.

	Archangel	Order of Angels
Kether	Metatron	Chaioth he Qadesh (Holy living creatures)
Chokmah	Ratziel	Auphanim (Wheels)
Binah	Tzaphkiel	Aralim (Thrones)
Chesed	Tzadkiel	Chasmalim (Brilliant ones)
Geburah	Khamael	Seraphim (Fiery serpents)
Tiphareth	Raphael	Malachim (Kings)
Netzach	Haniel	Elohim (Gods)
Hod	Michael	Beni Elohim (Sons of Gods)
Yesod	Gabriel	Cherubim (The Strong)
Malkuth	Sandalphon	Ashim (Souls of fire)

A word of warning: don't try and be clever and intellectualise about the nature of angels. Believe me, once you start working with angels you will have a better understanding of their nature. It's not for you or I to have a vague guess at their character; they will reveal it to you, all in good time.

As we have discussed, there is a school of thought that believes that your body can be represented as the Tree of Life (Adam/Eve Kadmon). If we believe this to be so, it will have all the attributes of the macrocosmic Tree of Life. It is logical to assume that, along with all the other symbolism, it will also come with its own set of ten archangels. The proposal is that it is possible to evoke your own archangels from within, so you are evoking the angelic part of yourself. Therefore interaction with angels can happen on a microcosmic (inner) level, as well as a macrocosmic (outer) level. So, if you are looking for your own Holy Guardian Angel, try looking inside yourself first!

The Temples

There are 32 paths on the Tree of Life, but if you study the image of the Tree of Life you will only find 22 connecting paths between the Sephiroth. So where are the other ten paths?

The answer is simple, if not a little sneaky. The first ten paths are the Sephiroth themselves, and are not strictly speaking pathworkings, but experiences. You travel a path but experience a Sephirah. To help you experience the Sephirah, each of the ten Sephiroth has a temple dedicated to it.

The exterior design of these temples can differ widely depending on the type of pathworking involved, religious conviction, etc. If, for instance, your pathworking is influenced by your empathy with the Norse tradition, the outer appearance of the Temple of Yesod would perhaps be a grand wooden Viking mead hall with all its associated carvings of dragons and other mythological beasts.

If, on the other hand, if you follow the Christian path, the Temple of Yesod might appear as a lonely stone chapel overlooking a moonlit Sea of Galilee.

The temples of the Sephiroth can be found in many different localities, from sea-tossed islands to rose-scented gardens. Normally the exteriors of the temples are fashioned by the paths that lead to them.

Conversely the interior designs of the temples remain much

the same, imbued by the nature of their particular Sephirah, and not influenced by the paths leading up to their doors. It is the power inside the temple that has authority on the paths outside, and not the other way around.

One thing all the temples have in common is a single sacred lamp burning on the altar. (As well as the one lamp on the altar, Netzach has a further seven lamps to represent the seven planets.) If the temple lamp is missing or not lit, you have wandered into the wrong place, a bad place. Throw a six and return immediately back to Malkuth, using the buzz word of power: *Adonai Ha Aretz*.

Feminine Sandalphon
With Double cube altar

Figure 11. The sacred lamp on the double cubic altar. [Combined with fig. 10, p. 40]

I have already described the Temple of Malkuth in Foreword. Malkuth, along with the remaining three temples on the Witches' Pyramid, will be made known to you as you work your way up the paths. Each temple shares the same divine name of power as its Sephirah. Again it would do no harm to familiarize yourself with the below list:

- Temple of Malkuth: Adonai Ha Aretz (Lord of the Earth)
- Temple of Yesod: Shaddai El Chai (The almighty living Goddess/ God)
- Temple of Hod: Elohim Tzabaoth (Gods of Hosts)
- Temple of Netzach: Jehovah Tzabaoth (Lord of Hosts)

As well as the angels, there are also many classical Gods and Goddess imbued in the fabric of the Tree.

Over the years most of the Gods and Goddesses of the mainstream religions both ancient and new have found a place on the Tree of Life. As we move into the future more are being added yearly, as fledgling cults and religious movements emerge.

As this book is aimed at teaching witches, who have an affinity with the old Gods, I have not included the Gods of contemporary patriarchal religions. The list below is made up from the more prominent classical Gods and Goddesses from the so-called Golden age.

There are of course countless deities I could list, particularly from the Egyptian pantheon. Because of this, my first list was a bit ambitious, so what I have given you is a much slimmed-down version. But, for the time being, I think this is enough to be getting on with. Again, read through them and assimilate the knowledge.

If you don't have fun, the gods won't come!

Goddesses and Gods Associated with the Sephiroth

	Egyptian	Roman	Greek
Kether	Nut	Jupiter in role of Sky Father	Zeus in role of Sky Father

5. Angels and Temples

	Egyptian	Roman	Greek
Chokmah	Amun	Faunus	Pan
Binah	Isis	Juno	Hera
Chesed	Osiris	Jupiter in role of City Father	Poseidon
Geburah	Horus	Mars	Ares
Tiphareth	Ra	Apollo	Apollo
Netzach	Hathor	Venus	Aphrodite
Hod	Thoth	Mercury	Hermes
Yesod	Shu	Diana	Artemis
Malkuth	Nephthys	Ceres	Persephone

6. Malkuth to Yesod – the 32nd Path

Having read the previous five chapters you will no doubt be keen to start your pathworking.

In this chapter you will enter the Temple of Malkuth and pass through the tarot card 'The Universe'. You will then travel up the 32nd path to the silver doors of the Temple of Yesod. Then, using the words of power "Adonai Ha Aretz", you will return safely back to the Temple of Malkuth.

The 32nd path will be your first experience of pathworking. Once you leave the Temple of Malkuth the path will transport you down into the Underworld before you can rise up to the higher astral plane.

The 32nd path at its lowest point drops down into the first level of the Qlippoth. (The Qlippoth is the hypothetical reverse side of the Tree of Life - its evil twin if you like.)

Here you will find the empty shells of what were once living things: vile husks of evil creatures stripped of their divine spark, which would have returned to the ocean of spirit from which it came, like a drop of rain returning to the sea. But what remains of their once-distorted beliefs and evil deeds falls into the abyss.

They say that to rise you must fall, so your first step on the Tree of Life is to encounter your negative side, to glimpse the dark side of your being before you are lifted up towards the light.

In the second part of the 32nd path, the initiate is shown the vast astral sea, which is under the domain of the Moon and models itself slavishly to the desires of Angels and Man alike.

Above the surface of the Astral Sea you are shown the planet Saturn with its attendant nine moons. Saturn demonstrates restriction through the principle of time. Above Saturn is the vault of heaven, where one can observe the machinery of the Universe, moving in perfect motion.

In the final part of the pathworking you embark on a ferry ride to an island on which stands the Temple of Yesod.

In Greek legend the souls of the dead were transported by Charon the ferryman across the River Styx to the Underworld, ruled over by Hades and his consort Persephone. The practice of placing a coin in the mouth of the deceased was so that the newly departed could pay the ferryman for their safe passage across the poisonous waters of the Styx. It's interesting to note that the River Styx is said to circle the Underworld nine times. And nine is the number of Yesod and the Moon. Interestingly the planet Saturn has nine moons also.

Writing about the River Styx brings to mind the legend of Greek goddess Persephone. Persephone is the bride of Hades, and as the ruling Queen of Hell also has her place on the 32nd path.

Persephone's Story

The ancient Greek legend tells of a powerful Earth goddess called Demeter, who had a beautiful daughter called Persephone. Demeter jealously guarded her daughter against all male suitors both human and divine, hiding her away in remote locations.

One late summer's day Persephone was innocently collecting flowers in a secret meadow along with some Nymphs, Oceanids to be exact, when suddenly Hades rose up from the Underworld through a crack in the rocks. He then abducted Persephone, dragging her down into the Underworld.

Once there, Hades seduced the virgin Persephone and set her up as Queen of the Underworld. Back on the surface nature came to a standstill as the devastated Demeter searched the face of the world for her daughter.

Finally the Sun, who sees all, told Demeter that Hades had taken Persephone down into the Underworld. By this time the land was laid bare and the people were starving, so Zeus intervened, ordering Hades his brother to send Persephone back to her mother.

But Hades had sealed Persephone's fate by tricking her into eating six pomegranate seeds. Anyone who eats or drinks in the Underworld is doomed to stay there for eternity, but to make Persephone happy and appease Zeus, Hades allowed Persephone to spend six months of the year with her mother Demeter, as long as she then spent the following six months with Him, reigning as Goddess of the Underworld (being one month for each of the seeds that she ate)

When Persephone reigns in the Underworld the land is barren (Winter), and when reunited with her mother the land flows with fertility (Summer). The lesson here is that, to appreciate the blessing of Summer, one must travel through the trials of Winter.

As Goddess of the Underworld, Persephone took to her role as Queen of Hades with relish, and got up to quite a bit of mischief of her own.

There are many interpretations to the Persephone story. But it's clear that the journey she made into the Underworld changed Persephone from a girl into a woman, innocent virgin to the dark Queen of Hades.

So Persephone travelled down into the darkness of Hades, only to rise up again to the sunshine, the green land, and the love of her mother. But the darkness called to her in the form of her husband Hades, so she returned for half of the year to rule by his side. She could not destroy the dark side of her nature but she could strive to master it. And mastering your dark side and conquering your deep-seated fears is one of the lessons of the 32nd path. It's interesting that the Greeks so feared Persephone in her role as Queen of Darkness that they dared not mention her name, so that they called her Kore instead, which means simply 'maiden' in Greek.

Figure 12. The Hebrew letter Tau.

6. Malkuth to Yesod – the 32nd Path

Before you start, meditate on the Hebrew letter Tau for one minute, then draw it a few times on a scrap of paper. This should fix it in your mind.

You will also need to be fully familiar with the tarot card 'The Universe', sometimes called 'The World'. You will need to visualize this card to enter the 32nd path.

As you know, there are many tarot packs in circulation today, and most are not suitable for serious magical practice. Sadly their symbolism has drifted so far away from the original meaning that they would not suit our purpose.

I strongly recommend the Rider-Waite pack, as it's a solid working pack and it's the one most commonly used for pathworkings. Another iconic pack is Aleister Crowley's Thoth pack, which is very potent with a touch of spiciness. The tarot of Marseilles is also a charming old pack, and the original symbolism is surprisingly accurate.

Start your pathworking by performing the Cabbalistic Cross, which will balance up your energies and cleanse your aura.

After you have completed the Cabbalistic Cross, construct the temple carefully in your mind's eye. You will find this easier than you anticipated. The temple is firmly built on the astral plane and will present itself to you without too much trouble.

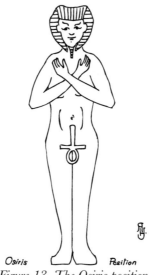

Figure 13. The Osiris position.

Figure 14. The tarot card 'The Universe'.

The Temple of Malkuth and the 32nd Path

The Temple of Malkuth stands on a raised dais. The floor of the temple is constructed from black and white flagstones, much like a chessboard. Around the edge surrounding us in a circle stand ten massive black pillars shot through with gold. Beyond the circle of pillars floats a thick white mist obscuring further vision.

In the centre of the temple stands a double cubic altar, upon which burns an open lamp, in light of which glitters off a small golden sickle laying nearby. Pick up the golden sickle: you will need it later.

As you look up, you see the pillars soar high above us, their tops hidden in a violet haze. Right in the centre there is a small break in the clouds through which twinkles a single star.

We are drawn back to the white flame upon the altar, and as we gaze deep into its heart, the flame begins to grow larger and larger, until it takes on the form of the female Archangel Sandalphon.

Sandalphon is dressed in the colours of Malkuth: citrine, olive, russet, and black. Her snow-white wings are folded neatly on her back. We relate to the Angel that towers before us and she blesses us.

After a while she stretches out her right arm and points to something behind us, in the east. We turn to look and to our amazement we see, floating between the pillars, three tapestries embroidered with three tarot cards: 'Judgement', 'The Universe', and 'The Moon'. The central tapestry, 'The Universe', glows with an inner light and we advance towards it. We stand and gaze at the picture. Each corner sports one of the four holy creatures of the elements; an angel, an eagle, a bull, and a lion. Inside a large oval of laurel leaves is a naked dancing female figure holding two wands. We are already familiar with this image as it's the 21st tarot key, `The great one of the night of time', or to give it its more common title, 'The World'.

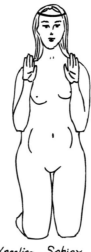

Kneeling Sphinx ♄.

Figure 15. The Sphinx.

We make the sign of the Sphinx: hands placed on our shoulders with palms facing front (see diagram). We repeat out loud the words 'to know, to will, to dare, and to keep silent' and place our index finger on our lips. As we do so, the oval in the centre of the card is blacked out and shimmers like the surface of a black mirror. As we gaze into its depths the woman re-emerges, and beckons us to enter the realms of Saturn, the dark one. We drift through, and suddenly we fall down into a sea of darkness. The darkness seems to thicken as we fall, slowing our descent. Eventually our feet touch solid ground and we stumble forward and take a few steps. The going beneath our feet is rough and uneven. As our eyes become accustomed to the darkness, we see strange elemental shapes that flit about us.

There seems to be a dim yellow glow filtering through the gloom some way in front of us. We stumble forward towards the light, and using our sickles we cut through thick fields of putrid weeds composed of corpses and decaying matter. Gradually the light builds in strength; lancing its way through the darkness towards us, it gives us strength to fight through this dreadful darkness that surrounds us. The going gradually becomes easier, until we come upon a hollowed-out glade bathed in golden light. A large solid Hebrew Tau stands in the centre, and its golden surface gleams and vibrates with earthy power. We place our hands on the Tau and feel the power of the earth pour into us. As the golden energy flows through our veins we start to feel strangely lighter. Soon our feet have left the ground and we are floating upwards between the tall columns of dark weeds that seem to stretch upwards to infinity, and faster and faster we rise. The way is getting lighter the higher we go, until in a burst of silver spray we break through the surface of the Astral Sea. We come to a halt hovering over the shining still waters.

We look around us at the vast sea, then up at the night sky above us. The planet Saturn with its bright rings hangs in the sky, and we count its nine moons. Above Saturn is the whole Universe in motion, the stars ebbing and flowing constantly in perfect balance. (Saturn is the God of time: without movement there would be no such thing as time.)

Turning our gaze once more to the Astral Sea we see a long, low, black barge coming toward us. Standing at the stern is a tall cloaked figure working a single oar. The barge comes to a halt directly beneath us. We float down and sit on one of the wooden boards that act as seats, and the barge immediately moves off in the direction from which it came. After a while, we come to a small island, upon which is built a simple white round temple which glows with a violet silver light. It has an aura about it which shifts and shimmers like the Moon sailing in and out of the clouds, and great power radiates from it. The barge rides the surf to land on a beach of fine silver sand. Miraculously we find that our sickles have changed into golden coins. We place our coins on the seat for the fer-ryman. We climb out of the prow of the boat and walk up the beach towards the temple. It's nice to feel the sand shift beneath our feet.

The doors to the temple are wrought of polished silver, with no sign of a door handle or key hole.

If you wish to enter the Temple of Yesod, you must intone the words of power, "Shaddai el Chai", and the doors will swing open.

However this time you must return to the Temple of Malkuth. To do so, just utter the words "Adonai Ha Aretz". The island along with the Temple of Yesod fades, and in its place forms the Temple of Malkuth once more.

The floor of the temple is constructed from black and white tiles, and ten black pillars, shot through with gold, stand around you. In the centre of the temple stands a double cubic altar, and the sacred lamp burns with a steady flame. Take a deep breath, and as you exhale let the temple fade and disappear. After your working it's a good idea to ground yourself with a little food and drink.

The old magical principle 'To know, to will, to dare, and to keep silent' is echoed in the four holy creatures depicted in the four corners of the tarot card 'The Universe', sometimes called 'The World'.

- The Eagle: To Know (ability to soar to heights)
- The Bull (Ox): To Will (patience and perseverance)
- The Lion: To Dare (strength and courage)
- The Human: To Keep Silent (spiritual wisdom)

Put these four beings together and you have the image of the Sphinx.

7. Yesod to Hod – the 30th Path

In this chapter we will explore the Temple of Yesod and the 30th path.

The 30th path leads the initiate away from the dreaming allure of Yesod to the crystal clear sharpness of reasoning thought found in Hod.

On this path emotional outbursts of love and anger are mastered, and the mind is disciplined, ready to embrace more intellectual pursuits. On this path you welcome the great centres of learning into your life, and turn your back on lewd physical pursuits.

One such centre of knowledge located on the 30th path is the 'BIBLIOTHECA ALEXANDRINA' (the Library of Alexandria).

The library was founded in Alexandria in Egypt in the third century BCE under the patronage of the Ptolemaic dynasty. Famed for its collection of ancient manuscripts and scrolls, it was celebrated by scholars throughout the ancient world. Disaster struck centuries later when Julius Caesar accidentally burned down the library when ordering the bur-ning of his own ships to deny their use to his enemies. Apparently, the fire spread from the ships to the docks, and then, unfortunately, to the library itself. Nevertheless, a substantial part of the library's collection survived the fire and was added to over the years, until the Muslims sacked the city in 642 CE and the library and its ancient contents were utterly destroyed.

In recent years, the library of Alexandria was placed on the 30th path as part of the pathworking experience. Strangely, the library has taken on a life of its own on the path between Yesod and Hod, bringing its sacred knowledge from the past into the future. The library of Alexandria now holds the Akashic records along with all its other treasures, and it is accessible by way of the 30th path.

It stands as a living example of the importance of setting down knowledge in scriptural form for future generations to read. Keeping notes and records is the essence to all learning.

Some people strive for immortality through their works. The desire to be famous drives them on to create great works of literature, art and music. The Egyptians thought that carving their name in stone would keep their essence alive. This is why new Pharaohs would have former rivals' names defaced, to deny them their eternal life.

Let's have a look at the 30th path before you travel up it. The walled garden seen in the tarot card 'The Sun' alludes to the Garden of Eden, and the naked male and female children are Adam and Eve. Although the garden is a safe and secure place to play as children, it restricts intellectual growth by keeping one innocent and therefore blind to the greater universe beyond its boundaries.

The circle in the grass is a fairy ring, and this, like the garden, can trap and impede intellectual development by flights of fancy. The fairy ring can also be a gateway to the 28th path, 'the path of myth and legend'. On the Tree it's mirrored on the right hand side leading to Yesod.

The strange birds are ibises, symbolic of the Egyptian god Thoth, god of writing and learning. (The patterns made by flocks of birds in flight can form divining letters in the sky).

The golden eggs are a nod to the mysteries of the Philosopher's Stone. The sun shines its rays into the garden, opening your eyes to the sunflowers that lean over the wall watching you. Your sudden desire to leave the garden initiates an act of will which illuminates the gate by which you can leave the garden. Mazes in ancient times were used for instruction and initiation, so as you travel towards the centre of the maze of sunflowers, your mind meditates on the mathematical puzzle set by the maze and shuts out emotional thoughts.

The snake in the maze could be symbolic of the serpent of wisdom, but can also represent the sexual power of the Kundalini.

At the centre of the maze stands the library of Alexandria which holds the Akashic records. And, like the ghosts from Dickens' Christmas Carol, they show things past, things present, and things yet to come. The twelve lecterns represent the twelve signs of the zodiac, which mark the twelve stations of the Sun, marking out our solar year. Astrology was very much an instrument of science in the earlier period of human development, and like the tarot card that shines light on the path, the Sun also lights our way to knowledge throughout our life. The books on the lecterns also show us the twelve Ages of Man. Having now left the Age of Pisces behind us, we are currently in the Age of Aquarius. Each age lasts about two thousand years. The beginning of the Age of Pisces heralded the coming of Christians in the west. The Age of Aquarius is newly arrived, and I wonder what it will herald?

It is inside the halls of the library of Alexandria that you find the door to the Temple of Hod.

Before you undertake the 30th path, it is important to meditate on the Hebrew letter Resh for at least one minute and then draw it on a scrap of paper, which should fix it in your mind. Also meditate on the tarot card 'The Sun' for one full minute before continuing further. Before you start your pathworking, perform the Cabbalistic Cross, which will balance up your energies and cleanse your aura.

Figure 16. The Hebrew letter Resh.

Figure 17. The tarot card 'The Sun'.

The 30th Path

The start of the 30th path begins at Yesod, so you have to travel there from Malkuth. You have two options. The first option is to simply travel up the 32nd path from Malkuth to Yesod.

The second option is to use your Adam/Eve Kadmon exercise to elevate your conscious mind up to Yesod, which activates the ten Sephiroth of your microcosmic body. Once you have done this, concentrate your mind solely on your Yesodic zone and let yourself be enveloped by Yesodic energy. See yourself enveloped by a bubble of violet light. Then simply float up between the black pillars of Malkuth until you reach the silver doors of the Temple of Yesod. Step out of the violet light and enter the Temple of Yesod, as if from a psychic elevator.

A word of warning: only use the second option, the psychic elevator, when you are proficient at working the 32nd path.

The 30ᵗʰ Pathworking

Visualise the Temple of Malkuth and build it up carefully in your mind's eye, uttering its name of power as you do so: "Adonai Ha Aretz".

If you wish to step though the tarot card 'The World' and travel up the 32ⁿᵈ path, follow the instructions laid out in Chapter 6. Otherwise, use your psychic elevator.

The Temple of Yesod is built on a small island which is surrounded by a wide, calm sea. The temple is fashioned in the shape of a short round tower. Its walls are smooth and chalk white. Set into the walls is a pair of silver doors. Walking up the sandy beach we stop in front of the silver doors and say the words of power, "Shaddai El Chai", and the doors swing open.

We enter the Temple of Yesod, which is larger on the inside then it appears outside. The inner walls are round and built from white marble. Standing away from the outer walls is an inner circle of nine white pillars shot through with silver and violet. The floor is inlaid with tiles of deep blue. Passing through into the inner circle of columns, we discover a round pool raised up from the floor and filled with midnight blue water. You can see the Moon reflected in the surface of the water, but looking around the temple you can see no sign of the Moon. The Moon only appears as a reflection in the surface of the pool, and its phase changes each time you visit the temple: sometimes an enchanted crescent like Diana's bow, sometimes full and bewitching.

Floating just above the water is a silver dish, from which rises the Lunar flame. As we stare into the heart of the flame, it quivers and grows into the form of the Archangel Gabriel, the messenger. His great wings of violet and silver are folded across his back. We look into his deep green eyes and have a vision of the sea, and the temple is filled with the sound and scent of the sea as if we were standing on a lonely beach at midnight. Gabriel's face shines in welcome, then raising his right hand he points to three tarot cards that have appeared between the pillars behind us. We thank Gabriel, turn, and move over to the tarot cards. From left to right they are 'The Sun', 'Temperance', and 'The Star'. These are the keys to the 30ᵗʰ,

25th and 28th paths, but it's the one on the left we need, 'The Sun'.

We look at it more closely. The card is illustrated with bright colours and is dominated by a large golden Sun wearing an indifferent look on his face. Hebrew Yods fall from the Sun. Below is a wall made from coloured stone blocks, and in front of the wall are two naked children playing in a fairy ring.

The heads of sunflowers look over the wall.

As we gaze at the scene, it becomes three dimensional; the children are images of ourselves when we were young. Holding out their hands they beckon us into the card. As we pass into the card, they disappear and we replace them in the garden. We explore our new surroundings. The garden consists of a green lawn with a flower border around the edge. It's early morning and the Sun has just risen and there is the smell of dew in the air.

There is a small fairy ring in the centre of the lawn dotted with tiny meadow flowers. As we step into the fairy ring we hear the tinkle of far off laughter, and taking each other's hands we do an impromptu dance around the circle.

We break off when two strange birds stalk out of the undergrowth and strut around the perimeter of the ring: they look like cranes. As we look on they both crouch down in the grass and lay a small golden egg each. Then without so much as a backward glance they stand up and disappear back into the undergrowth.

We have a strong compulsion to pick the eggs up. On doing so, the heavy but still warm eggs change into golden crossbows in our hands!

We notice again the large sunflowers looking over the wall into the garden. The ring is suddenly illuminated as the Sun rises above the heads of the sunflowers. We also notice for the first time a small garden gate set in the wall. Feeling it is time to leave, we open the garden gate and follow a narrow path which cuts its way into the ranks of sunflowers, and many paths branch off to the left and right. We soon realise that we are in a maze. We travel along a curved path for a while until we reach a dead end. It's very hot between the ranks of sunflowers, for the Sun has climbed high enough to shine down directly upon us. Irritably we retrace our steps until we come upon a round clearing with many paths leading from it.

We are just wondering which path to take when, to our dismay, a many-coloured serpent slides out from the thick stalks and rises up before us, blocking our way. The snake lifts its head about to strike, and we quickly aim with our crossbows and let the bolts fly. (The crossbows fall through our fingers like gold dust.)

The serpent straightway bursts into a column of flames. As the flames die down, in its place stands a golden Resh. We move over to this powerful Hebrew symbol and place our hands on its cool, smooth, golden surface. As we do so, we feel the power of divine intellect flowing through us, and understand clearly that we are in a mathematical maze, and to reach the centre we must keep to the left-hand side of the sunflowers. This we do, walking through the narrow ranks of tall sunflowers. We seem to be climbing steadily as we go, and all we can see is the Sun blazing in a blue sky and the heads of the sunflowers towering above us.

Taking a final right turn we break free of the sunflowers and find ourselves on the summit of a large, gently sloping hill. Standing directly in front of us on the summit of the hill is a building of great beauty. It is classical in structure, like a Greek temple. Wide steps lead up through eight massive pillars of white marble holding up a triangular fascia, on which is carved 'BIBLIOTHECA ALEXANDRINA' (The Library of Alexandria).

As we climb the steps to reach the entrance, we look behind us, across the ocean of yellow sunflowers that surround the hill, to the pastoral lands that lay beyond, the horizon lost in the golden haze of the midday Sun. Passing between the pillars we reach a pair of tall, wooden doors, which are wide open.

We pass into the great hall, and it feels pleasantly cool after the sun-baked steps outside. Inside, there are many splendid statues of famous teachers placed around the walls. If you visit the library often, perhaps you will hear them speak.

The floor is set with a fine mosaic set out in the form of the astrological heavens.

Behind the statues are shelves containing hundreds of ancient scrolls. In front of these, and running down each side of the hall, are rows of wooden lecterns. Sitting on the top of these plinths are large, ornately bound books that look like church Bibles. Six stand down each side, making twelve in total.

These books embody the twelve signs of the zodiac, or the twelve Ages of Man. In each reincarnation you are guided by the personality of the sign you are born under. The Sun travels through the twelve signs of the zodiac, and like the Sun your immortal soul travels through each of your incarnations, experiencing the best and worst that they have to offer.

Pausing in front of one of these books we notice that our astrological sign is engraved on its cover. Opening the book we look at the first page, but we see nothing but space, infinite space! As we look, a spark of light appears in the centre and grows into a large star. We know this is our Sun, and around it comes into being the solar system. We watch each planet in turn as it comes towards us, keeping its place in the great dance. Turning over the page, we see a child playing with a toy. The child is ourselves: are we looking into our own past?

Before we can see any more, the book silently closes on its own. Slightly alarmed we try to reopen the book but find it locked.

(We can use these books if they let us! They will show us living pictures that will enable us to see the ways in which man has gained his knowledge, and also the misuses to which he has put that knowledge.)

Turning our attention from the book, we look around us at the many scrolls and manuscripts that line the wall, wondering at the great knowledge they must hold. The library of Alexandria was only destroyed on the physical level: here on the 30th path, on the higher mental levels, it still exists. We feel an impulse to walk to the far end of the hall, where we discover between two bookshelves a small lintel door frame in the Egyptian style, into which is set a door that seems to be made of ice.

On the door is carved the Caduceus, the symbol of Mercury. Could these be the doors to the Temple of Hod? We utter the words of power, "Elohim Tzabaoth" – and yes, the doors swing slowly inward.

We find ourselves inside a large temple. There is a circle of eight pillars made from light red marble shot through with gold, so when your eyes move across their surface they appear orange. In the centre of the temple stands a waist-high stone altar of great antiquity, flanked on either side by a pillar of fire and a pillar of water.

On the altar burns the sacred flame. The floor is made up of intricate geometric patterns. We are fascinated by the ever-moving pillars of fire and water, and as we watch them the energy from the pillars seems to stretch out to each other and briefly touch. For a second, fire and water are fused together as one, forming a veil between the two pillars. The veil vanishes in a flash, and standing behind the altar is Michael, Archangel of Hod, 'the Prince of Splendour and of Wisdom'. He holds up his hand and blesses us.

The great Archangel then points behind us to the outer ring of eight pillars, and hanging there are three tarot cards. Two will guide you out of the Astral triangle up through the veil, and on up the Tree; the third will direct you horizontally across the Tree to Netzach. The first two are 'The Hanged Man' and 'The Devil'; the third is 'The Tower'. However, this time you must return to the Temple of Malkuth. Turn and thank Michael, utter the words "Adonai Ha Aretz", and then visualise the Temple of Malkuth once more.

The floor of the temple is constructed from black and white tiles, and ten black pillars, shot through with gold, stand around you. In the centre of the temple stands a double cubic altar, and the sacred lamp burns with a steady flame.

Talk a deep breath, and as you exhale let the temple fade and disappear.

8. Hod to Netzach – the 27th Path

In this chapter you will enter the Temple of Hod and traverse the tree using the 27th path until you reach the gates of the seventh Sephirah Netzach.

In the middle of the 27th path you will encounter 'The Tower', sometimes called 'The House of God.'

The tower used in context with the pathworking symbolizes three main concepts.

First, it represents the Biblical Tower of Babel built by man to reach up to heaven. God was less then pleased at the prospect of unwanted guests so he cursed the builders so that each and every one of them spoke a different language. As nobody could understand one another, the tower was quickly abandoned.

And the god of man is an angry god?

Secondly, it represents the towering ego of the initiate and their personality, built brick by brick from the moment they were born. To raise to a higher plane the initiate must have their personality knocked down or certainly modified, to allow a new temple to rise from the ashes of the old.

Finally, it symbolizes the phallus. Masturbation or sexual union leads to orgasm (lightning bolt). The ecstasy of orgasm is to unite briefly with the divine only to quickly fall back into reality. On the body of Adam Kadmon the erect phallus would cross the 27th path, suggesting that sexual power is on the same footing as spiritual grace when attempting to assail the abyss. The act of circumcision has also been suggested when in some packs the tarot card shows just the top of the tower being removed.

The balanced way to consider the tower, I believe, is to see a little of all three explanations built into its ramparts.

Some Thoughts on the Path

On leaving the Temple of Hod you first enter a chapel dedicated to recording humanity's technical and scientific progress.

There are eight scribes symbolic of the number of Hod. The saffron robes also tell us they are Hodic in character. One of the lessons of the path is to master your own ego: "Yes, you could argue that you are semi-divine, but you're not a God or Goddess yet."

The fall from the top of the tower is designed to humble you, so when you enter the Temple of Netzach you do so with modesty and the proper respect for the awesome power contained therein. The wolf eating up the heavens is called Fenrir, and is one of the children of Loki. On the day of Ragnarok (the Doom of the Gods), Fenrir will swallow the stairs and devour the mighty Odin along with Thor, Freyr and several other major Norse Gods. In this last great battle the world is drowned in water, only to re-emerge more fertile and beautiful than ever, but without the Gods.

At the end of the path there is a second chapel containing seven monks. In contrast to the first chapel, instead of recording science they are recording works based on human emotions.

Figure 18. The Hebrew letter Pe'.

Figure 19. The tarot card 'The Tower'.

Meditate on the tarot card 'The Tower' for one full minute before continuing further. It's important to meditate on the Hebrew letter Pe' as well, so draw it on a scrap of paper. This should fix it in your mind.

The 27ᵗʰ Pathworking

Start at the Temple of Hod, via the 32ⁿᵈ and the 30ᵗʰ paths, or more directly straight up the 31ˢᵗ path. Your third option is to use your Adam/ Eve Kadmon exercise (see Chapter 3). In short, activate the eight Sephiroth on your body, then envelope yourself in the energy of the Hodic zone (right hip). Again you should not use the psychic elevator until the relevant paths have been mastered, i.e. 32ⁿᵈ, 30ᵗʰ and 31ˢᵗ.

Once there, you will find the doors are made of ice that glows with an orange light. Touch the doors, say the words "Elohim Tzabaoth", and they will swing inward. Inside the temple are eight outer pillars set in a circle, made from red marble shot through with gold, so when your eyes move around the temple they flash orange. In the centre of the temple stands a waist-high stone altar of great antiquity, flanked on either side by a pillar of fire and a pillar of water.

On the altar rises the sacred flame. The floor of the temple is made up of intricate geometric patterns. The energy from the pillars seems to stretch out to each other and briefly touch. For a second, fire and water are fused together as one, forming a veil of steam between the two pillars. The veil slowly disperses and standing behind the altar is Michael, Archangel of Hod, called 'The Prince of Splendour and of Wisdom'.

Michael points to the other ring of eight pillars. Hanging there are three tarot cards. Two will guide you out of the Astral triangle up through the veil, and on up the Tree; the third will direct you horizontally across the tree to Netzach. The first two are 'The Hanged Man' and 'The Devil'; the one you need is 'The Tower'.

(The passage below takes the traveller through to the 27th path and on to Netzach.)

We stand before the tapestry of the Tower (The House of God).

The scene on the card is one of destruction. A storm-buffeted tower stands in the centre of the card, its summit being ravaged by lightening; two figures fall from its battlements, a King and a Queen, and many Hebrew Yods also fall to the ground with them.

The picture fades back into a blue icy glow, the card becomes transparent, and through it we can see a rough wooden door. Suddenly the ice veil lowers to the floor, changing as it goes into a freezing white blue mist, which creeps around our legs to vanish behind us. Looking at the door more closely we see placed in the centre is the eye of Horus, the centre of the eye fashioned from a deep red ruby. The ruby shines bright for a moment, then the door swings open to reveal a mediaeval chamber.

Eight monks stand at easels, clad from head to foot in their saffron habits. With white swan quills in their hands they carefully work on their illuminated manuscripts.

As we enter, one of the monks rises from his labours and bids us welcome. We ask what the monks are working on so diligently, and he answers: "We are recording what scientific truth mankind has discovered."

We feel slightly puzzled, but walk around the eight easels and examine their work. Each manuscript shows one of the universal truths that mankind has rediscovered. One shows a detailed map of our own solar system, all beautifully illuminated in a mediaeval style. Each manuscript shows what man has discovered about himself and the universe he moves in. "This is recorded on a higher level, so if Man was to fall back in ignorance due to a world war or religious hysteria, Man's past knowledge would be accessible to the future initiates," says the monk.

We thank the monks for their time and bid them continue their work in peace, telling them we must be on our way.

At the far end of the chamber is a large wooden door studded with nails. The two monks nearest the door rise to open it, and bidding them farewell we walk through. On the other side of the door, it is a beautiful summer's day. We are standing on top of a small hill overlooking a little valley, in the centre of which nestles a small village. The village is surrounded by a stream, or could it be a moat. It looks like the fair is in town. On the opposite side of the valley rises another green grassy hill, similar to the one on which we now stand. There is a building on its summit, a small round Tabernacle with cypress trees growing about it, keeping it company. We guess rightly that it must be the Temple of Netzach.

We decide that the best way to reach it is through the centre of the village, so we make off down the path towards the village. We are soon on the outskirts of the village. As the village is surrounded by a moat, the only way to enter the village without getting wet is over a stone bridge. However, the bridge appears to be a toll bridge. A toll man sits in a little stone niche set into the wall on guard. As we step onto the bridge the man steps out and bars our way.

"You may not perambulate farther along the path: first you must prove that you're intellectually superior to me," says the toll man.

The man then starts to brag about his knowledge of things magical, telling us all about the Tree of Life, gabbing on. We know that what he is telling us is the truth, but he's saying it so quickly and in such a mixed-up fashion that what he says does not follow any aim or point, other than to blow up his own ego and try to make us feel stupid. We soon get bored, and looking into the idiot's face for a moment, we find his face looks much like our own! The truth is brought home to us: how many times have we tried to impress others with our supposed superior knowledge? And we feel ashamed.

The toll man is so involved in himself that we just ignore him and walk across the bridge unmolested.

The village is mediaeval in style, and it is the day of the market fair. There are people everywhere, all gaily dressed in colourful costumes.

We walk up the centre of the cobbled main street. There are booths on either side: flea markets, amusement arcades, Gypsy fortune tellers. Many beribboned folk full of merriment dance in the street. A large brown bear on a golden chain dances around and around, led by a small mean-faced boy. "Dance, or it will be the worse for you; I'll pull your ears off," sneers the boy. The bear looks at the boy, terrified, and dances around all the quicker. "So often the strong are enslaved by threats backed up only by a sharp tongue", says a tall stranger, who is dressed in a harlequin costume. We think of all the times in our life when we have been that bear, and that wretched boy too, if it comes to that!

The stranger bids us to follow him, which we do. There are many stalls, swings and roundabouts, but, best of all, right in the middle of the town square is a magnificent brightly coloured helter-skelter. "Why don't you all climb to the top; you can see things more clearly from there," says the Harlequin. And with that he disappears into the helter skelter, through a mouth-shaped doorway fashioned like the Hebrew letter Pe'. We follow the Harlequin through the opening into the body of the tower. Inside, there are many levels leading to the top, each level lit by a small slit in the canvas. The inside holds scant resemblance to the gaily painted exterior: inside it is dull, flat, faded, and full of dust and cobwebs. Old wooden steps tied together with rope lead up to each level. As we climb up, we look out of the slit windows in the canvas: we see many truths about our own lives. (When we are born, we are like new leaves breaking from the bud to greet the spring sunshine, but the older we get, the more cluttered up inside we get.) Finally we come out into the fresh air at the summit. There waiting for us is the Harlequin. He speaks: "It is now time for you to see how great you have grown. You are no longer mere mortals: look around you!"

From the top, the tower appears much higher. Looking down at the village below, the carnival colours mark out the shape of a huge pentagram. The stream around the village forms the circle, and the four bridges mark out the four elemental quarters! "Yes, the magic circle, and you stand at the summit. You have only to say that you are Lord or Lady of all! Speak your wishes, and all can be possible," says the Harlequin.

We look out of this magic circle, past the boundaries of the village to the shimmering glories of the world.

We also look deep inside ourselves to access our lives, our loves, our hates, our dreams, our fears. We have only to say the word to change what we don't like.

We are tempted, but having walked two other paths on the lower triangle, we know deep down that once you change one thing, all things change. We know now not to tarry but be on our way as quickly as possible. No sooner have we decided on this course of action than a shadow runs across the land and the Sun is setting. As the Sun vanishes, below the hill we are plunged into darkness. Looking up, we see stars form and twinkle in the night sky. High up in the heavens one star shines brightest of all.

The surrounding stars start to revolve around this central star. There goes the Great Bear, and opposite the Little Bear. The Milky Way runs across the sky like a soft phantom. Suddenly, thunder rips the night sky and black clouds rise up from the horizon, forming themselves into the ghostly shape of a wolf's head with a gaping mouth. The Wolf spins around the night sky, swallowing up the stars, leaving nothing but the vivid darkness.

Soon the whole night sky is swallowed up except for that one central star. As the jaws of the great Wolf close on this last star, lightning flash-

70

es, lighting up the top of the helter-skelter. The Wolf's head reels back and suddenly a second bolt of fiery lightning flashes from the heavens, this time hitting the top of the tower. We are thrown off our feet and fall down and down, around and around! We are sliding down the helter skelter. As we slide down, the darkness is thrown out of our bodies, the scene about us is getting lighter, the sky is blue once more, and the hills that fly by are emerald green again.

Then suddenly, with a bump, we are at the bottom, and there to help us to our feet is the Harlequin. The village is much the same as we left it.

"You have done well," says the Harlequin, and with a wave of his arms he takes on the form of the Archangel Michael. Then, lifting his wings in a blaze of many-coloured flames, he is gone!

We quickly walk through the crowded streets to pass out of the village through the opposite side, leaving the music and the merriment behind us. Crossing the bridge, we find a semi-naked lad with a quiver of arrows on his back. He is sitting on the bridge's wall swinging his legs and writing something on a scrap of paper. Stopping, we ask him what it is he's writing. "I'm writing love poetry," he says. "Who to?" we ask. "To my muse; perhaps I'll write a poem to you," he sighs. "I'm in love with love, you see. I am just waiting for someone to come along so I can enslave them with love, for my poems have the power to hold many from their path for the longest time. Let me read some to you." Quickly we draw a line between ourselves and this God of Love. We hold our fingers to our lips and he falls silent, and he carries on with his writing as we go on our way.

Making our way up the opposite hill we stop and look behind. In the valley the village looks small and unreal, like a model, and there right in the centre is the colourful tower of the helter skelter, its colours flashing in the summer sunshine. It looks so small and harmless from here.

Walking on up the little chalk path, we finally reach the little temple we spotted from the other side of the valley. It is set in a garden surrounded by tall cypress trees. The garden is full of colourful wild flowers, rose briars hang off the scatterings of ancient garden ornaments, old busts of heroes and classical Gods mixed in with stone pillars and bird baths.

71

The scented blooms nod in the warm breeze. Seven hooded monks in dark green habits sit at easels, working amongst the delights of the garden of Netzach. Like their brothers from over the valley, they are recording things on illuminated manuscripts. They work with great tenderness, with large, black, Raven quill pens. Not the works of science, but the words of the great romantics: Hans Christian Andersen, William Blake, Shakespeare, and many more.

A monk at the far side of the garden stands up and walks across to us, hand held out in greeting. We notice straight away that the figure is that of a young woman; the cowl falls back as she walks to us, revealing a mop of golden red hair and a young shining face. "Welcome friends," she says. "The way through is now open to you."

Standing in the centre of the garden is a small rose-covered temple shaped like a little round summer house, built in the classical Roman style. The roof is made from red Roman tiles; seven classical pillars of light green marble with the finest veins of blue and red crystal running through support the roof. A flock of white doves perch on its roof, and there is a small arched doorway in which a small door nestles. The door is made from beaten copper, with a green emerald set into a star fixed to the centre of the door.

We have only to utter the words of power for the doors to swing open: "Jehovah Tzabaoth". If, however, you wish to return to the Temple of Malkuth, utter the words "Adonai Ha Aretz" and visualise the Temple of Malkuth - and you will be there. Remember that if you are ever in difficulty on any of the paths, just vibrate the words "Adonai Ha Aretz". This will bring you back to the Temple of Malkuth, and from there to your normal consciousness. This is the Tree's safeguard.

9. Yesod to Netzach – the 28th Path

Ignorance is bliss; it is folly to be wise.

The 28th path will lead you from Yesod to Netzach. This is a path influenced by the dreamy Astral world of Yesod and the highly emotional, sensual world of Netzach.

Many Pagans and romantics alike base their life on the energies of this path, for this is the path of legends and romantic myths. Here is J.R.R. Tolkien's Middle Earth, C. S. Lewis's Narnia, King Arthur and his sleeping knights. Hidden deep in this path are all the mysteries of Fairy Land, wild music and dance.

The devil said: "Music is the only thing that truly humbles me."

The positive side of myths and legends can inspire the heroic side of your nature to achieve great goals in life. The Arthurian legends tells tales of chivalry and heroic battles fought between good and evil. These examples, brought into practice in the everyday world, have been a force for good.

However, if the initiate decides to live a life based on fantasy and myth and turn their back on the real world, they will never move forward spiritually. They will be trapped in fairy rings of their own making. Remember that seeing castles in the sky is fine, but don't try and move into them.

On a more positive note, this path deals with Fairy Land and the supernatural spirits and beings that inhabit it. Such creatures can be found at ancient sites such as lonely hill forts, haunted woodland glades, old straight paths, ruins of old churches and abbeys. Fairies, elves, leprechauns, pixies, and will of the wisps are all common to those who wander abroad at night. Ghostly animals and phantom hares and horses, sometimes ridden by the little folk, haunt the misty moonlit fields that surround the country villages in the more remote parts of Britain.

This path introduces the traveller to the strong folklore traditions still very much alive in the British Isles today. Fairy stories inspire mystery and wonder, which is no bad thing in a world which too often can be regimented and humdrum.

Figure 20. The Hebrew letter Tzaddi

Figure 21. The tarot card 'The Star'.

74

Meditate on the tarot card 'The Star' for one minute before continuing further. You will also need to visualise the Hebrew letter Tzaddi clearly in your mind's eye, as you will encounter it somewhere in the middle of the path. As before, draw the symbol on a scrap of paper until you know it off by heart.

The start of the 28th path begins at Yesod, so you have to travel there. You have two options: the first is to travel the 32nd path from Malkuth to Yesod. The second option is to use your Adam/Eve Kadmon exercise.

In short, activate the ninth Sephiroth on your body and envelope yourself in the energy of Yesod, thus elevating your consciousness to Yesod. Then you simply step out of the violet light and you are there; it's our old friend the psychic elevator.

Before you start the meditation perform your Cabbalistic Cross exercise.

Next close your eyes and start.

The 28th Pathworking

As we walk up the sand towards the Temple of Yesod, a violet mist hides the path beneath our feet. In front of us stand the silver doors of Yesod. We say the magic words "Shaddai El Chai", and the doors swing open.

We enter the Temple of Yesod. It's larger on the inside than it appeared outside. The inner walls are round and built from white marble. Standing away from the wall is an inner circle of nine white pillars shot through with silver and violet. The floor is inlaid with tiles of deep blue. Passing through into the inner circle of columns, we discover a round pool raised up from the floor and filled with midnight blue water. Floating just above the water is a silver dish from which rises the Lunar flame. As we stare into the heart of the flame, it quivers and grows into the form of the Archangel Gabriel, the messenger. We relate to the archangel; he smiles, then points to his left. Between the pillars of Yesod hang three tapestries decorated with the colours and designs of three tarot cards. The one on the left is 'The Sun', the one in the middle is 'Temperance'. The last card, the one on the right, is called 'The Star', which is the key to the 28th path. Looking at the card you see pictured a large star with eight points (the points of the compass). Surrounding the large star are seven smaller ones, also octagonal in design. Below the stars is a fertile landscape with a pool of water in the foreground; snow-capped mountains lie on the far horizon. A naked young woman, half-kneeling, dominates the scene. Her left foot is placed firmly on the dry ground, whilst her right foot rests upon the waters. In each hand she holds a large urn from which she pours the Waters of Life. The water cascades from both urns, irrigating both land and sea with the divine power of the spirit. The water from the urns seems to wash away the colour and substance of the card from the base up. Behind the picture is a simple white wooden door with a silver star set in the middle.

We walk over to the door and touch the star, which shines brightly for a second, and then the door swings slowly open.

We pass through and find ourselves standing in an Italian-style walled courtyard. The cool flagstones beneath our feet feel nice to walk on. Placed around the walls are large Greek urns from which grapevines grow. The ancient vines climb up and around the walls; bunches of ripe grapes hang temptingly from their boughs.

The courtyard is cut in two by a shallow stream of water that passes through it. It runs in and out of the courtyard via two low arches set into the bottom of the walls.

On the other side of the stream stands a beautiful rowan tree, bedecked with shining red berries. We all have a strong desire to pick some of these bright red fruits, but first we must cross the stream. Its bed is made up from clean brightly-coloured pebbles, and we paddle into the refreshing water which is crystal clear. As it washes over our feet it seems to draw all tiredness and fatigue from our bodies, leaving us feeling refreshed and well. Stepping out of the water we walk over to the rowan tree. Reaching up we pick a bunch of red berries, which to our surprise untangle into a necklace of rowan berries, which we place around our necks - remembering that we heard somewhere in our past that the rowan is a great protection against black magic and evil enchantment. Looking around to get our bearings, we find to our amazement that the stream has gone and in its place is a wide, lazy river, its opposite bank lined with woodland trees of many kinds.

A swan glides up the river towards us. As the swan approaches, we see that it's too large to be a real swan; it's a wooden boat lovingly fashioned to resemble a swan. Standing in its wooden tail feathers is the slender figure of an Elf dressed all in greens and browns, busy manoeuvring the boat towards us using a single oar. The swan boat pulls up gently beside the river bank, and the figure beckons us to step in. The swan sways gently as we climb aboard. With a couple of quick movements of the oar, the Elf moves the swan out into the main stream of the river, then turns the boat against the current.

The boat moves so easily, with hardly any effort at all on the part of the oarsman standing in the rear, and glides gracefully upstream.

The river winds its way deep into the green wood, getting narrower as it goes. There in the trees by the water's edge we see a Unicorn! It dips its head, horn and all, into the water for a drink. Suddenly it realises we are watching it, and bringing its head out of the water it shakes the water from its golden mane in a shower of silver drops. The Unicorn looks at us for a moment, then with a swish of his tail turns and trots back into the trees. The boat goes on its way. Looking across the river to the other bank, we spot two Centaurs in a woodland clearing. One has a brown, curly beard and hair to match; his horse's body is a powerful chestnut steed.

In contrast, the second Centaur could not be more different! A female with a beautiful, elegant body, she has milk-white breasts and golden hair with a garland of flowers crowning it, and her body is a slender, white dappled mare. As we watch they turn to face one another, hold hands and kiss. Taking no notice of the boat, they start caressing each other's hair and ears, and we watch enchanted.

As the boat moves up the river, we quickly lose sight of them. The Elf tells us that "Only through love can their animal and human nature come together and understand one another," and we try to understand this lesson.

The swan boat glides on up the river until it comes to a wooden landing stage. The oarsman pulls up alongside it, then jumps across onto the jetty and moors the boat. We all take our leave of the swan boat and thank our oarsman for the ride. A wide woodland path leads up from the river bank into the woods. The woods are full of pools of green light as the sun filters through the foliage high up in the canopy. The air is heavy with the scent of trees and leaf mould.

We look around and breathe in the atmosphere. Shortly we come to a large clearing. There are lots of elves, both male and female, dancing, feasting, and generally making merry: it seems to be a festival of some kind.

In the centre of the clearing stands a white hawthorn tree which is growing in the shape of the Hebrew letter Tzaddi. Its leaves are emerald green and it is studded with hawthorn blossoms (little milk-white flowers that smell like a woman's Yoni). Just in front of the hawthorn tree is a long table set with food and wine, and sitting at the head of the table are the King and Queen of Fairy Land.

"Come my friends, eat and drink with us. Drink from the cup of forgetfulness; it will wash from your minds the worry and torment of your journey through life. Forget strife! Stay with us forever!" laughs the King.

But we know that to take food and drink in Fairy Land is to make a pact with Fairy Land, and one would not be able to leave as easily as we came. Already the way we came is barred to us and the only way back is to go forward, so we say to the King and Queen "We dare not eat with thee, but we will make a toast to you, and the Lord and Lady of us all." We each take one of the delicate little chalices from the table, but, before we put the cup to our lips, we squeeze a little drop of juice out of one of the rowan berries that hang around our necks. This action causes the King and Queen to give us a look of admiration. "We see that you are indeed children of the wise. Let us drink now to the Lord and Lady of the world and drain this sweet wine."

"Why do you travel through our domain?" ask the King and Queen.

"The path of initiation takes us this way," we answer.

"We will help you on your way," says the Queen, and, taking a small wooden whistle from her jewelled, studded belt, she gives a long, clear note.

Straight away, a herd of ponies come running into the clearing. They are no ordinary ponies: these have wings, like the fabled Pegasus, sprung from the blood of Medusa. "These are fairy steeds, and they will help you on your way," says the Queen.

Quickly we climb up on to their backs, and the fairy ponies run across the clearing. Then, they stretch their wings out, and we sweep up into the air, just clearing the tops of the trees. Higher and higher we fly; looking down, the woods seem far below us. Before us in the distance are snow-capped mountain peaks. We pass over many lands, fair lands with fairy castles with golden towers and spires.

The mountains are straight ahead now, and as we gain more height, we fly up into the snow-capped citadels. There is a green glow on the western horizon, and the winged ponies fly swiftly towards the green light. As we get closer, we can see that it is not a star but a green glow that is lighting up the clouds like a Chinese lantern. Reaching the clouds we plunge straight into them, and all around us now is green mist. As our ponies descend, we suddenly burst out of the green mist. Below us is a large apple orchard, and we swiftly land and dismount. The ponies jump into the air and fly around us. Sensing that they wish to return to Fairy Land we bid them farewell, and with a low pass they fly back into the clouds.

We stand for a moment, looking at the golden apples which hang from the trees. A warm breeze blows across our brows, bringing with it the scent of roses.

We decide to follow the smell. Weaving through the trees we discover a large rose garden. Standing in the centre of the rose garden is a small rose-covered temple shaped like a little round summer house, built in the classical Roman style. The roof is made from red Roman tiles. Seven classical pillars of light green marble, with the finest veins of blue and red crystal running through, support the roof. A flock of white doves perch on its roof. There is a small arched doorway in which a small door nestles. The door is made from beaten copper, with a green emerald set into a star fixed to the centre of the door.

To enter the Temple of Netzach, knock on the door and say the words of power - "Jehovah Tzabaoth" - and the door will open.

The inner Temple of Netzach is warm and full of provocative scents. The pillars support a domed roof of white marble with a hint of rose white. On entering the temple, we look around us and see in the centre a small classical altar with its sacred flame burning on the top. Above us there is a smoke-hole set in the middle of the ceiling, and painted around the hole is a seven-pointed star with a lamp hanging from each point on a slender chain. These are the Seven Lamps of Power.

The floor plan mirrors the ceiling, except that at each point of the star is set one of the signs of the seven planets, all inlaid into the floor using a colourful marble mosaic, with the Altar acting as the centrepiece. As we look into the flame on the Altar, a bright rose-coloured light fills the temple, and from this light emerges Haniel, the female Archangel of Netzach, called the Princess of Love and Harmony. She is dressed in long, flowing robes, and her hair is the colour of burnished copper held in place by a circlet of red roses.

She blesses us, then speaks to each of us in turn. When she is ready to depart, she hands each of us a rose from her circlet. We thank her, and with a smile she disappears. We feel a strong impulse to place the rose into the sacred flame as an offering to the Gods. The rose is quickly consumed by the flame, releasing a thin line of rose-coloured smoke that rises up to escape through the hole in the ceiling.

When we are ready to leave the Temple of Netzach, we simply shut our eyes and vibrate the words "Adonai Ha Aretz". We open our eyes to find ourselves back in the Temple of Malkuth.

10. Malkuth to Netzach – the 29ᵗʰ Path

Whatever terrors may assail the mind,

the answer is the same at every stage:

"How splendid is the Adventure."

The 29ᵗʰ path runs from Malkuth to Netzach. This path deals with the darker side of the Moon's nature, filled with fear and superstitions. Sometimes called 'The path of the Red Moon', it is full of unbridled sexual urges, bestial and lustful, which can lead in turn to sexual guilt and remorse.

Aleister Crowley in his Thoth pack connects 'The Moon' card with the menstrual cycle, when the womb is emptied and the blood flows to make ready to receive the chance of new life once more. This time in a woman's menstrual cycle was seen as taboo in many early tribal societies. Even today in some parts of the world women are still ostracised by the men of the tribe, their natural cycle seen through superstitious eyes. The path also deals with the phases of the Moon, and the uncanny way a woman's menstrual cycle often mirrors the lunar month.

The 29ᵗʰ path helps the initiate to understand the powerful sexual urges that can assail the personality and wipe out reasonable action. Sexual action can be a plague or a blessing; its ultimate goal is to bring about new life, but on a human level it also brings pleasure and cements relationships between partners. This path takes the initiate on a journey from primeval sexual lust to the romantic rose arbours of the lover-poet.

The path is ruled over by Pisces. The 'two fishes' motif of the sign is represented by the twin dolphins at the start of the pathworking.

In the Temple of Netzach the seven lamps represent the Seven

Lamps of Power, each associated with one of the seven classical planets: Sun, Moon, Mercury, Venus, Jupiter, Mars, and Saturn. To take one down is to imbue you with its power, but beware: you wish to direct the power of the lamp and not become a prisoner inside it. See 'Aladdin, Genie of the lamp'.

Figure 22. The Hebrew letter Qoph.

Figure 23. The tarot card 'The Moon'.

Meditate on the tarot card 'The Moon' for one minute before continuing further. Draw the Hebrew letter Qoph several times before you begin your pathworking, so that you can visualise it with ease. As always, before you start your meditation perform your Cabbalistic Cross exercise to put you in balance and cleanse your aura.

The 29ᵗʰ Pathworking

We find ourselves standing in a large temple. The floor is constructed from black and white flagstones, much like a chess board. Surrounding us stand ten black pillars, shot through with gold. Beyond the circle of pillars is a thick white morning mist obscuring further vision. In the centre of the temple stands a double cubic altar, upon which burns a brass lamp.

As we look up, we see the pillars soar high into the sky, their tops hidden in a violet mist. Right in the centre there is a small break in the clouds through which twinkles a single star. Looking at the white flame on the altar, we see that it is growing larger and larger, until it takes on the form of the female Archangel Sandalphon.

Sandalphon is dressed in the colours of Malkuth: citrine, olive, russet, and black. We relate to this figure. After a while she points behind us, and turning our heads our gaze follows her pointed arm. We see, hung between four pillars, three tapestries embroidered with three tarot cards: 'Judgement', 'The World', and 'The Moon'.

It is the one on the right that we are interested in, 'The Moon'.

The picture shows a bleak landscape with a pool in the foreground, out from which crawls a crayfish, drawn out of the water, no doubt, by the power of the Full Moon which hangs menacingly in the night sky.

A path leads up from the pool to pass between two dark towers that stand naked on the horizon. Two dogs stand guard on either side of the path.

Stepping into the scene on the card, we fall straight into the pool. Floating gently down through the waters we find ourselves in a warm subterranean water garden. This is a beautiful, colourful, tranquil place, full of all manner of marine plants, coloured corals and sea anemones. Shoals of sea-horses float by, and there are fish of every kind. Look there! An angelfish, and behind that stone a pink octopus, no bigger than your hand. We are in Neptune's garden, and there, seated on a throne made from mother of pearl tastefully studded with jewels, is the old King of the Sea himself, his beard swaying in the gentle current. In attendance are many beautiful sea nymphs. Mermaids and mermen swim around us, but they keep a discrete distance; each mermaid carries a mirror in one hand.

Neptune speaks: "This is your physical birthplace; it is from these briny depths that all creatures that walk on dry land have their origins. It is your heritage."

A strong current suddenly develops and pulls the subterranean flowers and plants this way and that. "It's the pull of the tides!" says Neptune.

"It's the Moon, you know, same thing twice a day. It was that same pull that drew life up out of the waters, many eons ago," he says.

"It is the force that you must follow today: I will lend you two of my favourite dolphins – they will act as guides".

The dolphins are summoned. We thank the King, and say farewell to the sea nymphs and mermaids and mermen. Swimming after the dolphins we manage to take hold of their dorsal fins. We travel swiftly through the salty water, and as we go the sea becomes cold and grey. Finally, our guides lead us to our destination, and breaking the surface we find ourselves in a moonlit cove. Thanking the dolphins for safely leading us through the seas, we wade through the surf up on to a sandy beach. We are not the only creatures on the water's edge: crustaceans of all kinds, crabs, lobsters, and crayfish crawl out of the surf up on to the beach. The Full Moon hangs low in the night sky, lighting up the scene in silver-grey light. We walk quickly up the sand and shingle to the scrubland some little way off. A large golden Qoph stands on the boundary between the seashore and dry scrubland. We gather instinctively around this mighty symbol that rules the path, and touching the Qoph for a moment we feel one with the sky, land, beach, and sea. We turn and gaze out across the sea, which is as still as a millpond, still and forbidding. Turning, we look up the path that leads up from the Hebrew letter, out across the rugged landscape directly away from the sea, heading, it seems, straight towards the Full Moon.

We walk silently along the path listening to the sounds borne on the night air - the chirping of insects, and the odd howl and hoot car-

ried on the night breezes. Suddenly a new noise interrupts our thoughts, the sound of hoof beats. Looking in the general direction from where the new sound is coming from, we see off to our right a ghostly white horse carrying a dark rider illuminated by the Full Moon. What's more, he appears to be galloping across the rough terrain in our general direction. We stand watching the rider as he crosses the path some way ahead, having now seen us! The shadowy rider swings his horse around and returns to the path, and is now trotting down the path towards us.

The horse and rider come to a halt directly in front of us, menacingly, blocking our way, and seemingly trying to force us off the path. We stand firm and hold our ground. The rider moves two steps forward: now he is standing right before us, blacking out the moonlight, and we are fully under our uninvited guest's shadow.

But, far from being frightened, our spirits are joyfully energised. The rider then throws back his cloak, bathing us in the glittering cold silver violet light! It is the Archangel Gabriel. Gabriel speaks: "To reach your goal you must pass through the twin towers of Superstition. Furthermore, to be able to pass through unmolested, you must give up all your cherished superstitions, such as walking under ladders, etc., and as a result you will be free of them forever." Gabriel wraps his cloak around himself, taking on the guise of the black rider once more, and with a quick word of farewell horse and rider turn and disappear under the shadow of some nearby bushes.

Contemplating the words of Gabriel, we carry on our way. The path starts to climb slowly. The two towers that Gabriel spoke of loom up before us, dark and forbidding against the pale moonlit sky.

As we approach, the Moon hangs between them like a large, luminous cheese. We have now reached the two dogs that stand on either side of the path, both baying at the Moon. The dog on the right is a rough-looking mongrel, and in the moonlight could easily be taken for a wolf or a coyote. The one on the left looks like a well-groomed house dog. Furthermore, he is wearing an expensive-looking collar around his neck. As we approach they ignore us: they are far too busy being mesmerised by the moon to pay us any heed. The Moon starts to take on a reddish hue. The dogs respond to this change by jumping up and down and howling in a most excitable manner, saliva dripping from their mouths. Each dog has a fully erect organ which secretes shining sperm, as they are both mad with lust and passion.

Looking up at the Moon we also feel deep sexual passions welling up inside our own bodies. As we stand looking through the twin towers at the Moon, we fancy that the dark towers are the thighs of the great mother, and the scarlet Moon her open vagina. With blood emanating from within, she is in her menstrual period, making her womb ready to receive new sperm so as to create life once more! We start to understand the great force that the Moon exerts on the sexual habits of all creatures living on the face of the Earth, ensuring fertility for all. (Having the ability to reproduce is one thing, having the drive to want to is the job of the Moon.)

As our own sexual urge strengthens, we know that we must move forward and pass through the twin towers of superstition. We walk between these two towering edifices: 'Their architect, falsehood; their purpose, to accommodate all manner of the superstitions that plague mankind'. The path as it passes between the towers is constructed from black, slippery cobblestones.

The towers at their bases are much closer together then one would first believe. As a result, as we walk the way gets narrower. In fact, if we stretched out our arms we could touch both towers at once. Not surprisingly it's dismal between the towers, and the sensation is one of clammy warm sweat. Nearing the end of the passage, we find to our dismay a black turnstile blocking our way. It is in the same style as the ones you would expect to find at the entrance to a seaside pier. As we start to examine it, out pops an old woman - a real hag, black-grey greasy hair, bent back, hooked nose, and all. "Who are you, and what do you want?" she cackles. We tell her. "If you want to pass through, you must first pay for the privilege," says the old hag.

"What do you require in payment, old woman?" we ask.

"Two things. First, all your personal superstitions that envelope you

in mind and body, which I will keep safely locked up in these fair structures!" she cackles!

"And second, a big kiss!"

We agree.

"Right" she says. "Say after me:

I will no longer be a slave to my superstitions."

"- I will no longer be a slave to my superstitions."

"For I have sold them to black Isis, for a kiss!"

"- For I have sold them to black Isis, for a kiss."

Coming through the turnstile, we each give the old hag a kiss. She whispers "Blessed Be", and, surprised, we return "Blessed Be".

The kiss was not so bad. In fact up close the old hag smelt quite fragrant, like a rose garden on a warm summer evening.

We walk through the turnstile and pass down into a far more ordered landscape, leaving the twin towers behind us. Our surroundings remind us of the garden of a stately home, lit of course by the ever present Moon. The Moon is now above us, riding high in the night sky like a large white pearl, with a few scattered stars for company.

On each side of the path are grey-green lawns, broken up by little ornate hedges, and odd clumps of shrubbery also line our way. Groves of cypress trees stand silhouetted in the moonlight, and best of all, the roses! Standing roses, rose bushes, rose trees, in fact roses everywhere you look. In addition to all this, there are statues dotted about. Some nestle in rose arbours, some in the centre of a lawn, all ghostly white, with one thing in common: lovers every one, taken from history or romantic literature. We look at them closely and notice their eyes seem alive; see how they look at each other, lost in their love. (Love is like the rose, beautiful and fragrant, but look out for the thorns thirsting for blood). It is said that the statues come alive on certain nights of the year, when the Moon is full and there's magic in the air. Perhaps one might climb down off their plinth to offer you a kiss, or something more.

As we walk on, a large privet hedge looms up directly in front of us, seemly blocking our path again. As we approach the hedge we see that there is an opening cut through it, acting as a living archway through which the path disappears. Looking through, we are dismayed to find yet another privet hedge standing behind the first. Then it dawns on us that this is not a boundary hedge at all, it's a maze!

We enter this labyrinth of privet, to be faced with our first puzzle: we can go either to the left or the right. Looking back and forth up the leafy corridors, the two ways are identical except for one thing. Down the right-hand passage there are red roses growing out of the hedge; by way of a contrast, white roses grow out of the hedge along the left-hand corridor. We make up our minds to follow the path of red roses. Our goal is still to reach the Temple of Netzach, and red roses symbolise love, so off we set.

Once inside the maze, we find wide hedged pathways and secret arbours containing ornate garden benches. The maze is warm-scented and seductive. We understand that this maze was not planted to confuse and trap, but to be a place where lovers can escape and meet in secret.

Finally we enter the heart of the maze, where a large rose garden bathed in moonlight is laid out in front of us. Standing in the centre of the rose garden is a small rose-covered temple shaped like a little round summer house, built in the classical Roman style. The roof is domed, and a flock of white doves perch on its roof.

There is a small arched entrance in which a small door of beaten copper nestles. In the centre of the door is an emerald set into a gold star. If you wish to enter the Temple of Netzach simply knock on the door and say the words of power, "Jehovah Tzabaoth", and the door will open.

The inner Temple of Netzach is warm and full of provocative scents. There are seven pillars of light green shot through with red and blue crystal. The pillars support a domed roof of white marble with a hint of rose white. We look around us and see in the centre a small classical altar, with its sacred flame burning on the top. Above us there is a smoke-hole set in the middle of the domed ceiling. Painted around the smoke-hole is a seven-pointed star, with an ornate lamp hanging from each point. These are the Seven Lamps of Power. (See Chapter 8 for more information.)

10. Malkuth to Netzach – the 29th Path

The floor mirrors the ceiling, except that at each point of the star is one of the signs of the seven planets, all inlaid into the floor using a colourful marble mosaic, with the altar acting as the centrepiece. As we look into the flame on the altar, it grows into a bright rose-coloured light in the form of a human being, which hovers above the altar. The shape materializes into Haniel, the female Archangel of Netzach, called the Princess of Love and Harmony. She is dressed in long, flowing robes, and her hair is the colour of burnished copper, held in place by a circlet of red roses.

She blesses us, then speaks to each of us in turn. When she is ready to depart she hands each of us a rose from her circlet. We thank her, and with a smile she disappears. We feel a strong impulse to place the rose into the sacred flame as an offering to the Gods. The rose is quickly consumed by the flames, releasing a thin line of rose-coloured smoke that rises up to escape through the hole in the ceiling.

When we are ready to leave the Temple of Netzach, we simply shut our eyes and vibrate the words: "Adonai Ha Aretz". Open your eyes, to find yourself back in the Temple of Malkuth.

11. The 31st Path – Malkuth to Hod

In the beginning was the word, and the word said, 'No.'

The 31st path runs from Malkuth to Hod. This path shows the power that fire has given humankind, and the uses we have put it to. To understand fire is one of the goals of the path.

There are many concepts connected with the idea of fire, for instance:

- "Fire in the brain." In the elemental man, fire is attributed to the head, air to the chest and arms, water to the stomach and loins, and earth to the legs and feet.
- "Keep the home fires burning." The idea of a warm fire waiting in the hearth for the returning solder was so popular in the Second World War that there was a famous song written about it.
- Goddess Vesta and the sacred fire of Rome. The practice of keeping a sacred light burning to dispel the darkness is as old as humankind.
- Fire festivals. These are celebrated throughout Europe and beyond. Beltane is a particular favourite of Pagans. For the general populace, Bonfire Night with its Guy and raucous fireworks is a chance for all to herald in winter.

This path tells of Man's rise through the use of fire, from ape to super ape, from cave-dweller to astronaut.

Pictured in the tarot card 'Judgment' is a grave or a tomb which opens up, so that humankind can rise up to the heavens. It speaks of the Ascent of Man. It's Michael, archangel of fire, who summons the figures out of the confinement of the tomb to their true destiny. The lesson of the path is to show the initiate just how important fire is, both spiritual and physical.

Prometheus and the 31ˢᵗ Path

Prometheus is ancient Greek for 'Forethought'. Prometheus was a Titan, or the son of a Titan. He was thought to be a champion of humankind. He is known best for stealing fire from heaven and giving it to humans. Prometheus is also known for his witty intelligence, and is credited with playing a crucial role in the early development of the history of humanity.

Prometheus was a thorn in the side of the Sky Father Zeus, and was always trying to find new way to confront Zeus's omnipotence. For example, a sacrificial meal was prepared at Sicyon to mark the settling of accounts between mortals and the Immortals (the Gods of Olympus). Prometheus felt that Zeus was too harsh on his human subjects, and played a trick on him. He placed two sacrificial offerings before the mighty Olympian. The first was a selection of bull's meat hidden inside the animal's stomach (nutrition hidden inside a displeasing exterior). The second offering was the bull's bones hidden inside a package of glistening white fat (something inedible hidden inside a pleasing exterior).

Accordingly Zeus chose the second offering, setting an example for future sacrifices. Henceforth humans would keep the meat for themselves, and burn bones wrapped in fat as an offering to the Gods. This so angered Zeus that he took back fire from the humans in retribution.

Not deterred, Prometheus sought an audience with Athena, and, after some flattering, asked her for admittance into Olympus. This she gladly granted.

On his arrival, Prometheus lit a torch at the fiery chariot of the Sun to light his way into the grand chamber of the Olympians. Before he entered he broke a piece of glowing ember off the torch, and thrust it into the pithy hollow of a giant fennel stalk he had stuffed in his belt. Once the audience was over, he extinguished his torch and stole away back to Earth and returned fire to humankind once more.

Once Zeus found out what Prometheus had done, he punished him. He ordered Vulcan to forge a chain of iron, and with this chain Prometheus was bound to a rock in the Caucasus. Each day a large eagle would swoop down and eat his liver, which would grow back overnight, only to be eaten again the next day.

It was the Greek hero Hercules that shot the eagle and set Prometheus free from his chains after a period of some thirty years. I suspect Zeus had a hand in this.

For the romantics, Prometheus was seen as a rebel who opposed all forms of institutional tyranny handed down by cold-hearted officialdom, epitomized by Zeus's domination of Olympus and the human world beneath.

Percy Bysshe Shelley wrote in his four-act play Prometheus Unbound a similar story to the one above, but swapped Zeus to Jupiter.

Mary Shelley's novel Frankenstein is subtitled 'The modern Prometheus'. The novel's theme is that man has over-reached himself in his pursuit of knowledge, and so created for himself a dangerous monster. This theme has become shockingly real in the creation of the atom bomb.

In the Disney film Jungle Book we see the ape king Louie kidnap Mowgli to gain man's red fire. It is clearly a reference to Prometheus and the theory that man evolved from apes.

The Archangel Michael and Prometheus are very similar in some respects: see the tarot card 'Judgement'.

Figure 24. The Hebrew letter Shin.

Figure 25. The tarot card 'Judgement'.

PROMETHEUS

Figure 26. Prometheus.

VULCAN

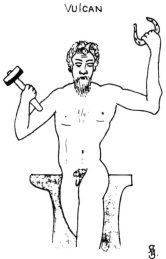

Figure 27. Vulcan.

Before you start your pathworking, meditate on the tarot card 'Judgment' for one minute before continuing further. Also draw out the letter Shin lots of times to get it in your head: you will need to visualise it once on the path. Make ready your space, perform your Cabbalistic Cross exercise, and then start your pathworking.

The 31ˢᵗ Pathworking

We find ourselves standing in a large Temple. The floor of the temple is constructed from black and white flagstones, much like a chessboard. Surrounding us stand ten black pillars, shot through with gold. Beyond the circle of pillars is a thick morning mist obscuring further vision. In the centre of the temple stands a double cubic altar, upon which burns a polished brass lamp.

Looking at the white flame on the altar, we see deep in its heart many coloured lights like the tiny lights on a Christmas tree. As we look on, they split from the flame and fly around the temple like many coloured fireflies.

These are the souls of fire, the Ashim. They fill the temple with a feeling of delight. Then, as quick as they came, they return to the sacred flame, which starts to build into a column of white light that transforms into the form of the female Archangel Sandalphon.

Sandalphon is dressed in the colours of Malkuth: citrine, olive, russet, and black. We relate to this figure, and after a while she points behind us. Turning our heads, we follow her pointed arm and see, hung between four pillars, three tapestries embroidered with the three tarot cards 'Judgement', 'The Universe', and 'The Moon'. It's the tarot card on the left that we need to travel the 31ˢᵗ path. Upon it is a pictorial representation of the 20ᵗʰ tarot card, 'Judgement'. The scene on the card is a seascape with three coffins floating upon its surface, in which stand three naked figures. The one on the right is a man, the one on the left a woman, the one in the middle is a child. Above them in the sky is the Archangel Michael, surrounded by an aura of living fire. The card symbolises the end of one incarnation and the beginning of the next.

Alternatively, for the initiate it can mean that you have passed one initiation, and you are being summoned up to the next level.

The picture takes on a 3D effect. As we walk into it, the Archangel lifts up his fiery wings and the scene in front of us is lost in a supernova of coloured flames, which sweep over us so quickly as to do no harm. Our senses are full with the smell, sound, feel, and taste of fire. As our heads clear, we find ourselves standing in a large volcanic cave made of reddish rock. The air is hot with fumes and full of the sounds of boiling and hissing.

This could well be the Hell that the Christians talk about all the time, or on the other hand it might be one of the realms of Hades.

We walk slowly down the wide passageway, and as we go, the cave becomes quieter and cooler. The smell of molten rock and burning gas gives way to the sweeter smell of earth and damp stone.

The cave seems to have aged as we make our way through it: the rock that seemed newly formed, now looks and smells millions of years old. The red glow gives way to a dusky yellow light that seems to be filtering into the cave from somewhere up ahead. As we turn a corner we can see a little arch of daylight.

We move towards the entrance of the cave and notice, to our delight, cave paintings of animals and matchstick men hunting with spears decorating the walls of the cavern.

We examine the remains of a camp fire surrounded by flat stones, some of which have strips of dried meat lying on them. Piles of simple pottery stand against the wall: more evidence of the early use of fire.

Looking out of the mouth of the cave, we see a dry landscape with the odd stand of trees. A narrow, dusty path winds its way down from the mouth of the cave into the valley below.

The sky has an orange glow to it, which matches the terracotta tint of the soil. Dotted about in the valley are many large outcrops of rock, volcanic in nature. The small path leads us to one such rocky outcrop shaped like an ancient dolmen. Nestling under the shadow of the stones is a blacksmith's forge.

Working at the forge is Wayland the Smith, pumping animal skin bellows with one hand, and holding a spear point in the white-hot charcoal with the other.

Wayland is naked except for the scorched leather apron around his middle. Wayland works quickly, with amazing skill considering his primitive equipment.

"See how I make the sparks fly!" laughs Wayland. We ask him what it is that he is making. "A spear for hunting food. I also make spears to rend the earth to bring forth her bounty," says Wayland, pointing to an iron ploughshare.

"Remember that fire is a gift to Mankind from the Titan Prometheus. Fire opens the door to creative manipulation of the physical world."

We thank Wayland for his words of wisdom, and leave the smith to his labours. As we walk out of the forge , Wayland shouts after us: "Remember, fire makes a good servant, but a bad master. Fare well."

Leaving the smithy we continue to follow our little path. It's not long before we come to a golden letter Shin, which stands solidly in the middle *of the path and comes up to our chests. Something seems to motivate us to place our hands on its surface. It is smooth and warm to the touch, and vibrates in an odd way. We seem to have attracted a swarm of iridescent fireflies that proceed to dance about our heads. They then cluster together to form the figure of Michael, the Archangel of fire.*

"Follow me to the avenue of the singing fire," says Michael, pointing to some ancient ruins some way down the path. Michael glides down the path in front of us, his feet hovering just above the ground.

Approaching the ruins, we see two lines of stone rams in a crouched down position with their heads up and their mouths open. The stone rams form an avenue through which runs the path. As we enter the avenue, the air is full of the sound of whispering voices. Suddenly, a fireball shoots from the mouth of one of the rams. It flies past our head taking on the form of a mouth, and lets forth a string of unintelligible words as it flashes past. Then two more emerge and zip past. "These are the tongues of fire that speak the words of the Logos. It was these same tongues that taught the disciples to speak the languages of the world at the feast of Pentecost," says Michael. Silence for a moment! Then, a multitude of these fiery tongues seem to fill the avenue. The early whispering is now an angry roar, getting louder and louder.

Michael raises his wings of fire and the stone rams fall silent once more. "It's time to move on," says Michael, passing swiftly through the last pair of stone rams. We quickly follow, leaving the avenue of rams behind us. Once we are safely back on our path, Michael says farewell, and he ascends up into heavy, dark clouds that have gathered. The sound of distant thunder fills the air.

Looking down the dusty path that winds its way on through the arid landscape, we notice something strange starts to happen.

Soft rain drops descend from above to pockmark the dusty path. The rain seems to be confined to the small area in which we are standing. Then, rising up from the damp ground in front of us is a ring of cypress trees. Years of growth happens in seconds as the trees shoot upwards.

We enter the grove of cypress trees, and, to our surprise, standing in the centre is a large round stone temple with a domed roof. A pair of red cedar doors are set into the walls. The doors swing in silently to our touch. Entering, we find ourselves standing in a well-lit circular passage that skirts the outside walls. The decoration is Roman in style. The floor beneath our feet is tiled with a patterned mosaic. Pieces of Roman furniture stand against the walls of the passage.

We make the sign of silence, so we will not be seen or heard, for we are here to observe only. (Put your index finger to your lips.)

We then follow the curve of the passage. At the far side of the circular passage we pass through two open doors into the main part of the temple, where a sacred fire is tended.

The fire itself is right in the centre of the round chamber. There is a domed roof with a smoke-hole in the middle, out through which passes the sweetly-scented smoke. The fire is tended, night and day, by the Vestals.

As the hearth in the home gives light and heat to the family unit, so the sacred fire gives light and strength to the city state.

We stand and watch the women going quietly about their duties. Two tend the fire and two fetch fuel for the fire, which is usually faggots of wood from fruit trees, which will give off a sweet odour when burnt. The remaining two girls rest nearby, making six in total. Fragrant incense is sprinkled onto the flames. This sacrifice of time and devotion is given freely and with love.

Leaving the inner sanctum of the temple we return to the passage. Walking down the other side, we discover yet another set of doors set in the outer wall.

These doors are not Roman in style; far from it – these doors are made from black iron with two Chinese dragons fashioned on the front. The doors swing open to reveal a garden that is oriental in style. Wide steps lead us down into a beautiful garden. Numerous Chinese lanterns hang in the trees, ceramic dragons and tigers peek out from beneath the exotic plants and trees. The garden path leads us down to the edge of a large lake with an island in the middle, on which stands the saffron Temple of Hod.

Suddenly a rocket explodes high up in the sky above the Temple of Hod, and a burst of coloured stars lights up the sky. (The firework is the path's way of saluting you; it is also to be taken as a mark of respect.)

The light from the firework is reflected on the crystal-clear waters of the lake. We wonder how we can cross to the Temple of Hod: perhaps we could wade across or swim? Kneeling down by the water's edge, we touch the surface of the water with our fingers. Suddenly fire spreads from our finger-tips to race across the lake's surface like a mini tidal wave, causing the water to freeze behind it. We cautiously step onto the frozen lake and make our way over to the ice doors of the Temple of Hod. To enter the temple we have only to say the words of power, "Elohim Tzabaoth". If however you wish to return to the Temple of Malkuth say the words "Adonai Ha Aretz".

With the closing words "Adonai Ha Aretz", you have completed all six pathworkings on the Witches' Pyramid and have visited all its four temples. I sincerely hope that you will travel them often until you have built up a bond with the inner planes. In time you might like to write your own pathworkings to reflect your chosen spiritual direction. Remember, however, that all paths lead the true initiate to the middle temple of the sacred flame.

All the world's religions turn around this central point, and, like a great mill-stone, they will try and grind the last drop of devotion from you. Enjoy your religion but don't be a slave to it. Remember that all religious rituals are but humanity's attempt to court the divine. Find your own inner light and know yourself.

Afterword

I cannot finish this book without mentioning the Qlippoth, because the minute you mention the Cabbala someone will.

The Qlippoth is a dark mirror-image of the Tree of Life, like an inverted reflection on the surface of a black stagnant pool. Everything that's positive and good about the Sephiroth is mirrored in the Qlippothic tree as negative and evil. For example, all the vibrant life force in Malkuth, the wind through the trees, the music of birds on the wing, holding a loved one in your arms – gone! The Qlippoth offers only empty shells of the living, with all the life force sucked out of them. Instead of hope – despair, instead of love – the most cruel hatred.

Hope may die, but the hunger does not.

Malkuth is the only Sephirah on the Tree to touch the Qlippoth. In its four-colour combination of citrine, olive, russet and black, black is there to indicate that Malkuth is also a gateway to the Qlippothic Tree of Life. You briefly encounter it at the start of your 32nd path. Don't be tempted to follow that path down. As Robbie Burns puts it:

Don't look upon monsters,

lest you become a monster.

But even in the darkest recesses of hell resides the seed of light. So consequently, in the brightest spheres of heaven grows the seed of darkness.

This puzzle of Yin and Yang explains why things never go quite right in human affairs. The Universe is always in a state of change. The best-laid plans of mice and men, etc.

An interesting fact for you to ponder is this: the lowest point on the Qlippoth Tree is the Qlippoth equivalent to Kether, or the Qlippothic Kether if you prefer. It's like the epicentre of hell and its vice is atheism.

Bibliography

I have not burdened the text and pathworkings with endless references but, with great thanks, I acknowledge the inspiration and information gained from the following sources.

General
Crowley, Aleister, *The Book of Thoth*, Samuel Weiser Inc.
Gray, William, *The Ladder of Lights*, Helios.
Fortune, Dion, *Moon Magic*, The Aquarian Press
Fortune, Dion, *The Sea Priestess*, The Aquarian Press.
Knight Gareth, *A Practical Guild to Qabalistic Symbolism*, vol. 1 and 2, Helios.
Sturzaker. James, *Kabbalistic Aphorisms*, Metatron.
Wang, Robert, *The Qabalistic Tarot*, Samuel Weiser Inc.
Williams, Jean, Cox, Zachary, *The Gods Within*, Moondust Books.